MACBOOK
FOR SENIORS

The Most Complete Guide to Learn in Simple Steps
How to Interact with Your MacBook Air and Pro.

---

*With Illustrated Instructions and Useful Tips to Boost Your
Confidence with All the Features and Tools.*

GARETH MAYER

ABOUT THE AUTHOR

Gareth Mayer was born in the US. He was an IT expert and is now an entrepreneur with a passion for teaching. He believes technology can simplify elders' lives and help them feel less alone and more connected with their relatives and the world.

TABLE OF CONTENTS

CHAPTER 18: BEST PRACTICES FOR KEEPING YOUR MACBOOK SECURE

CHAPTER 1: INTRODUCTION

Macbook Air and Pro are ideal for seniors over 65 who want the latest technology in a powerful, reliable machine. It is easy to set up and provide access to applications that can help keep seniors connected with friends and family, including email, video chat, social media, and more.

Both models come with the macOS operating system, which is user-friendly and intuitive, so seniors can easily stay updated with technology. With its sleek design, powerful performance, and long battery life, a MacBook Air or Pro is perfect for staying connected with family and friends while on the go.

MacBook for Seniors is an ideal option for anyone who wants to stay up to date with the latest technology without going through a steep learning curve. With Apple's intuitive interface and easy-to-use software, it's never been easier for seniors to access their favorite activities. Whether you plan on using your computer for entertainment, staying in touch with family and friends, or managing your finances, MacBook for Seniors has you covered.

MacBook Air and Pro also come with Apple's support service, which is available 24/7 to answer questions and help with setup and troubleshooting. It makes it easy for seniors to get technical assistance if they ever need it. A MacBook has a one-year limited warranty covering hardware failures due to factory defects or faulty workmanship.

CHAPTER 2: THE DIFFERENCE
BETWEEN WINDOWS AND MAC

Seniors over 65 may find switching to a new computer system daunting, as they often have more experience with outdated systems. By understanding the key differences between Windows and Mac systems, they should be able to make an informed decision when it comes time to purchase a new computer. However, it's always a good idea to research both systems and speak with knowledgeable individuals before purchasing. Being informed and learning more about the available options can help seniors make the best decision for their unique needs.

When considering the differences between Windows and Mac systems, there are several key points that seniors should be aware of. A few of them are:

User Interface

The first difference is in terms of the user interface. Windows has remained largely unchanged since the early 2000s, with a desktop full of icons. At the same time, Mac offers a more modern look and feel focused on minimalism. It could make it easier for seniors to adjust to the new system if they are familiar with the Windows interface.

Moreover, Windows has a traditional desktop environment which can be cumbersome for seniors. In contrast, Macs have a more intuitive and streamlined interface that makes it easier to navigate the system. The docking feature of the Mac also allows users to access their favorite applications quickly.

Security

Windows has more security options than Mac, as there is an extensive array of antivirus and firewall software that you can install on the system. On the other hand, Macs are generally considered safer due to their built-in malware protection, so seniors may not need to worry about extra security measures.

Software

Another significant difference between the two systems is in terms of applications or software that you can use on them. The Windows system has many more options in terms of applications and software that you can use. At the same time, Macs are limited to only those developed by Apple. It could limit the options available for seniors accustomed to using certain applications.

There are many different types of software available for both systems, but Windows has a much larger selection than Macs. Despite this, Macs still have a good selection of software designed for seniors, such as senior-specific word processing and photo editing applications.

Hardware

Windows offers a greater range of hardware choices than Macs, making it easier for seniors to find a device that suits their needs. Many Windows devices also cost less than their Mac counterparts, which could be beneficial if a senior is on a limited budget.

Accessories

Many accessories are available for both systems, such as a mouse, keyboards, monitors, and hard drives. However, Windows is more compatible with external accessories, while Macs may require additional drivers or software to be installed.

Cost

Both systems can be expensive, but Windows is often cheaper than Mac due to the abundant discounted or bundled hardware and software available.

Compatibility

Due to the different hardware used by each system, seniors need to ensure that any peripherals or software they purchase are compatible with their chosen system. Windows has a much wider range of compatibility options due to its widespread use in PCs and laptops. In contrast, Macs have fewer but reliable compatibility options.

Reliability

Macs are known for their reliability and lack of viruses, while Windows often has more stability issues. However, both systems can also be prone to crashing due to faulty hardware or software. So, seniors must ensure their computer has the latest updates installed.

Upgrading

Macs are not designed to be upgraded or modified, while Windows provides more flexibility in terms of upgrades. It can benefit seniors who want to upgrade their system over time to keep up with the latest technology.

Support

It is often considered easier to troubleshoot windows due to its built-in support options and online resources available for users. Macs often require more technical knowledge to troubleshoot issues.

Battery Life

Due to the superior battery efficiency of Macs compared to Windows, seniors may find that their systems can last longer throughout the day without having to be plugged in. It is especially useful for seniors who need to stay productive outside the home.

Both Windows and Mac systems have advantages and disadvantages for seniors. Considering cost, compatibility, support, and battery life, seniors can make an informed decision that best suits their needs. It is important to note that whichever system they choose will require ongoing maintenance to keep their system secure and up to date. Ultimately, the best approach for seniors will depend on their individual needs and preferences.

CHAPTER 3: THE BENEFITS OF
USING A MACBOOK AIR AND PRO

Easy-to-Use Operating System

The MacBook Air and Pro are two of the most popular laptops on the market. They offer seniors an easy-to-use operating system that is perfect for all their computing needs. Both come with Apple's macOS (formerly known as OS X) software, designed to be highly intuitive and user-friendly. The wide range of features it offers makes it ideal for seniors who may not be as tech-savvy as younger generations.

The macOS operating system is designed with simplicity, and seniors will find it much easier to use than a Windows PC or laptop. The intuitive design and interface make navigating the computer easy and enable seniors to learn how to use their new device without confusion quickly. With many features and options available, seniors can customize their MacBook Pro or Air for their specific needs.

High-Quality Speakers

The MacBook Pro and Air both feature high-quality speakers. They provide great audio clarity allowing seniors to listen to music and podcasts or watch movies without connecting external speakers. The loud volume is perfect for those who are hard of hearing, and the sound remains crisp even when turned up to a high volume.

For seniors looking for high-quality speakers in their MacBook Air and Pro laptops, they will be satisfied. These powerful audio systems deliver a crisp sound with plenty of volumes to fill a room. They also have impressive features like noise cancellation technology that reduces background noise, so only the music is heard clearly. Plus, the built-in bass enhances low frequencies for a fuller, richer sound.

Long Battery Life

Another great benefit for seniors is the long battery life of MacBook Pros and Airs. With the latest models, including up to 12 hours of battery life, seniors can use their laptops throughout the day without worrying about constantly charging the device. This long battery life is ideal for those on the go and who need their laptop to last throughout the day.

Lightweight Design

MacBook Pros and Air's lightweight design makes them perfect for seniors who may have difficulty carrying heavier laptops around. With their slim and light designs, seniors can easily transport their MacBook from place to place without feeling weighed down.

Accessibility Features

For seniors who may have difficulty using a standard laptop, MacBook Pros and Airs have various accessibility features that make it easier for them to operate the device. From built-in magnifiers to voice control, seniors can easily adjust their MacBook to meet their needs and make using the laptop a much easier experience.

Security Features

A MacBook comes with various built-in security features that protect data from malicious threats. From secure password protection to encrypted storage, seniors will have peace of mind knowing their data is safe and secure on their MacBook Pro or Air.

Durability

Also, a MacBook is designed for longevity, and seniors can expect their laptops to remain in good condition for many years. The high-quality construction of the device makes it resistant to damage from accidental drops and everyday wear and tear, making it the perfect device for seniors who may not be as careful with their laptops.

Price

Finally, MacBook Pros and Airs have become much more affordable in recent years, making them an excellent option for seniors on a budget. With options to purchase refurbished models or secondhand laptops, seniors can get the same great quality of a MacBook at a fraction of the cost.

MacBook Pros and Airs are perfect for seniors due to their easy-to-use operating system, high-quality speakers, long battery life, lightweight design, accessibility features, and durability. With an affordable price, seniors can enjoy all these benefits without breaking the bank.

CHAPTER 4: BASIC TERMINOLOGY
AND FEATURES

The MacBook Airs and Pros are both excellent choices for seniors looking for an easy-to-use laptop with plenty of performance and portability. Apple has something to offer whether you're looking for basic computing needs or advanced functioning operations.

Both have been designed to meet the needs of seniors. Both laptops have various features that make them user-friendly for those over 65.

Basic Terms

The following are basic terminologies that seniors need to understand while using a MacBook:

App

This refers to an application or program you can use on the computer. Examples of apps include web browsers, media players, and word processors.

Apple ID

It is your user name for everything you do with Apple, such as using the App Store, iCloud, iMessage, FaceTime, and more. It's also the primary way to manage your Apple account and make purchases from the App Store.

Mac

Mac is short for Macintosh, a computer brand made by Apple. The latest Macs are powered by Intel processors and come in several designs, including laptops, desktops, and all-in-one systems.

Dock

The Dock is located at the bottom of your Mac computer's screen. It contains shortcuts to all the apps and files you use regularly. To view your Dock, move your cursor to the bottom of your screen. You can customize the Dock to contain only the apps or files you want.

Finder

Finder is the main application to navigate and manage your files and folders. It allows you to organize, access, and open your documents, pictures, videos, music, and more. To open Finder, look for its icon in the Dock.

Launchpad

Launchpad is a feature of macOS that provides an easy way to access all your Mac apps in one place. To open Launchpad, click the round icon at the screen's bottom-left corner. You can also access it using a four-finger pinch gesture on a trackpad or searching for "Launchpad" using Spotlight. From Launchpad, you can launch installed apps, delete apps and create folders to organize your apps.

Mission Control

Another handy feature is Mission Control which allows you to quickly view all open windows in one place. To access it, use the F3 key or swipe up with three fingers on a trackpad. It will group all your open windows, desktop spaces, and full-screen apps. You can also create new desktops from here to organize your work.

Menu Bar

Located at the top of your screen, this contains all the menus necessary to control and customize your computer. It includes options like System Preferences and About This Mac.

Spotlight

Use the Spotlight feature to quickly find what you're looking for on your MacBook. To access it, click the magnifying glass icon in the upper right corner or press Command-Space. Spotlight searches can include documents, contacts, applications, and more. You'll see a list of results appear in the same window – to open a result, click on it or press Command-Return.

Keychain Access

The Keychain Access feature is a secure way to store passwords and other sensitive information. It saves you time logging into websites, programs, and applications. To access Keychain Access, go to the Utilities folder in your Applications folder or search for it using Spotlight. From there, you can add, delete and modify items stored in your keychain.

Notification Center

The Notification Center keeps track of important information like calendar appointments, emails, and weather. To access it, click the icon at the top right corner of your screen or swipe two fingers from right to left on your trackpad. From here, you can enable notifications for specific apps and check out the Today View for a quick summary.

Siri

Siri is an intelligent assistant that helps you get things done quickly and easily. To activate Siri, click the icon in your menu bar or press Command-Space. Ask questions, set reminders, and more –talk to Siri as if you're talking to a friend. You can even ask it where to find specific documents on your Mac!

Safari

Safari is the default web browser for the MacBook. It allows you to browse websites, download files, and do more online.

AirDrop

AirDrop is a wireless technology that lets you quickly and easily transfer files between your MacBook and nearby Apple devices like iPhones, iPads, or other Mac computers. To use AirDrop, open the Finder window on your MacBook and then click the "AirDrop" icon in the sidebar on the left side of the screen.

Time Machine

Time Machine is an excellent feature of the MacBook. It's an automated system that backs up your files and stores them in an external drive or other storage devices. In that way, you can retrieve them if they get lost or corrupted.

By understanding these basic terminologies, seniors can easily access the features on their MacBook and make the most out of them. With practice and patience, using a MacBook may even become more enjoyable for them.

MacBook Air Specifications

The MacBook Air is ultra-light - weighing only 2.75 pounds - making it easy to take on the go. The laptop comes with a 13-inch Retina display, which offers sharp and clear visuals that are perfect for viewing photos or streaming movies. It also features an 8th-generation Intel Core processor and up to 16GB of memory to handle your needs efficiently. It also has a Touch ID feature, granting quick access to the user's account without typing in a pin or password.

MacBook Pro Specifications

The MacBook Pro, on the other hand, offers more power and storage options than the Air. It features a 13-inch Retina display with True Tone technology for an even brighter and more true-to-life viewing experience. The laptop is powered by an 8th-generation Intel Core processor with up to 16GB of memory and 2TB of storage. It also comes with the Touch Bar feature, which gives quick access to frequently used tools and shortcuts.

Both models are great choices for seniors looking for lightweight laptops that can handle all their computing needs.

Battery Life

The MacBook Air and Pro have long-lasting batteries lasting up to 12 hours. The Air also has excellent storage options, with the choice to upgrade to up to 512GB of SSD storage. The Pro offers up to 4TB of hard drive space, perfect for storing a large library of movies, music, or photos.

Operating System

The MacBook Air and Pro both feature the same macOS operating system, which offers an easy-to-use interface and a wide range of applications. They also provide wireless internet connections, allowing seniors to stay connected wherever they go.

Ease of Use

The Air is also highly portable due to its thin profile, making it perfect for seniors who travel often. It's also great for those that need to take their laptop with them for work or school. On the other hand, the Pro is better suited for power users who require more performance and flexibility from their laptops.

Cost

Seniors should also consider the cost of a MacBook Air or Pro. The Air starts at $1,099, and the Pro starts at $2,399, so it's important to consider your budget when making your purchase decision. Although they may be more expensive than other laptop options, Apple products are noted for their reliability and quality. So, if you're looking for a laptop that will last, an Apple MacBook may be worth the investment.

Ultimately, the Air and Pro models are great options for seniors who want reliable computer performance. It's essential to consider your needs when making your purchase decision to get the best laptop.

CHAPTER 5: HOW TO GET STARTED
WITH YOUR MACBOOK AIR AND PRO

Getting to Know Your MacBook Air and Pro

As a senior, you may have heard of the MacBook Air and Pro series but need help understanding how they differ. Both laptops are powerful and feature-rich, but a few key differences can help you decide which is right.

The MacBook Air is typically lighter, making it easier to carry around. It also has a longer-lasting battery life, so you can get more use out of your laptop without constantly charging it. The Air also features a 13" Retina display with True Tone technology for sharp, vivid colors that look great from any angle.

The MacBook Pro offers more powerful performance and higher graphics capabilities. It is an excellent choice for users who want to stream videos, play games, or do other intensive tasks. The Pro also has a slightly larger 15" Retina display and Touch Bar with Touch ID for added convenience.

When deciding which MacBook is right for you, consider how much portability you need, what type of performance you require, how long your battery needs to last, and which display features are most important. With the MacBook Air and Pro series, seniors can find a powerful laptop that fits their needs.

No matter which model you choose, the latest software from Apple, MacBook Air, and Pro offers seniors an easy-to-use and powerful laptop. Whether you're streaming videos, playing games, or need a larger display for web browsing and other everyday tasks, the MacBook Air and Pro are both great options.

CHAPTER 6: SETTING UP YOUR
MACBOOK AIR AND PRO

Once you have received your new MacBook, the first step is to ensure it's set up correctly so you can access all the applications available on the App Store. Here are some tips for setting up your MacBook Air or Pro:

Connect to a Wi-Fi network.

This will allow you to download and update apps from the App Store. To do this, click on the Wi-Fi icon in the upper-right corner of your screen and select your preferred network from the list.

Sign in With an Apple ID

An Apple ID is required to access the App Store. You can create an Apple ID by clicking on the 'Sign In' option from the App Store menu if you don't have one.

Install Useful Apps

Once you have signed in with your Apple ID, you can start browsing the App Store for useful applications. Many great apps are available that are designed specifically for seniors. They can be downloaded and installed with just a few clicks.

Get familiar With the Interface

The MacBook interface may initially seem complex, but it's very user-friendly. Spend some time getting familiar with the various menus and tools available on the laptop so you can easily access all the features.

Check for Updates

Check for updates regularly, as new versions of apps may contain important fixes and enhancements. To do this, open the App Store on your MacBook and click on the 'Updates' tab at the top. It will show all the available updates you can install to keep your apps up-to-date.

These are just a few essential tips for setting up your MacBook Air or Pro. With these steps, you can access the App Store and start downloading apps to help make your life easier.

CHAPTER 7: USING MAC OS

Logging In and Out

For most users, logging in to a MacBook Air or Pro laptop is relatively straightforward. However, seniors who need to become more familiar with computers may find the process more complicated. The following step-by-step guide will help seniors learn how to log into their Mac laptops:

1. Locate the power button on the keyboard and press it to turn the device on.
2. Once the laptop is powered up, you'll be asked to enter your username and password.
3. Type in your username and associated password into the fields provided and press Enter or Return on your keyboard.

4. If you successfully log in, it will take you to the main screen of your MacBook Air or Pro.

5. To log out of your laptop, locate the Apple logo at the top left of the screen. Click on it.

6. A drop-down menu will appear where you can select "Log Out."

7. Once logged out, you'll be taken back to the login screen, where you can enter your username and password again when needed.

Following these steps will ensure that seniors have a successful experience logging in and out of their MacBook Air or Pro laptop. By doing so, they can use the device more confidently and quickly. With some practice, seniors can become comfortable using this type of computer.

Creating and Managing User Accounts

Learning how to create and manage your MacBook Air or Pro user accounts can be a great way to ensure everyone's data stays private. It also allows you to control which programs and features each user can access. This guide will create and manage your MacBook Air or Pro user accounts.

First, you need to open System Preferences by clicking the Apple icon in the top-left corner of your screen and selecting "System Preferences." Once this window is open, select the "Users & Groups" option.

Once inside the Users & Groups page, it will present you with a list of current users. To create a new user, click the "+" icon in the bottom-left corner. It will open a window where you can enter the new user's name and password and select their account type.

Setting Up a User Account

Setting up a user account on the MacBook Air and Pro can be done in just a few simple steps.

1. Go to System Preferences, located in the Apple menu at the top left of your screen.

2. Select Users & Groups. Here, you will see all existing user accounts.

3. Click the "+" button to create a new user account.

4. Enter the new user account's desired name, password, and other information.

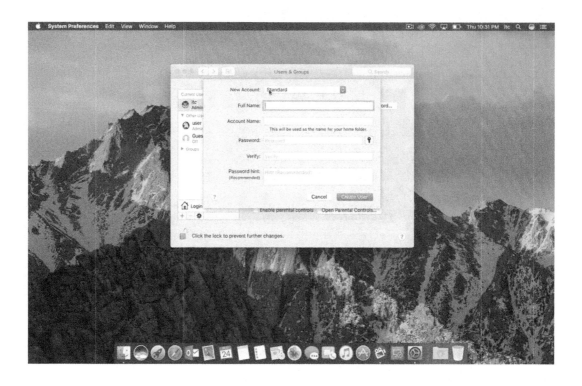

5. Select an image or avatar and click Create user to finish setting up the account.

6. Click the "Enable Parental Controls" button to set up parental control features.

7. Select an age range for the account and click OK to confirm.

8. You can now customize other settings, such as limiting access to websites, online store purchases, and applications from the Parental Controls tab.

9. When you are finished setting up a user account, click the "lock" icon at the bottom left of the window to save your changes.

This step-by-step guide will help seniors easily set up and manage their MacBook Air and Pro user accounts. With a few clicks, they can create new user accounts, customize access settings, and enable parental controls.

Note:

It's also important for seniors to remember to keep their usernames and password secure. They should not share it with anyone else or save it in an insecure location, such as on a sticky note. It's also essential to choose a strong password that is difficult to guess. Having a secure login will help protect the laptop from unauthorized access.

Creating an Apple ID

With an Apple ID, you can access the App Store or iTunes and buy apps, music, movies, and other online content. Here is a step-by-step guide on how seniors can create an Apple ID for their MacBook Air or Pro:

1. Open your web browser and go to https://appleid.apple.com/account
2. Enter your desired email address and click "Continue."
3. Enter a strong password for your account and select the security questions you want to answer if you need to reset your password.
4. Review Apple's Terms & Conditions and Privacy Policy, and click "Agree."
5. Enter your date of birth and click "Continue."
6. You will now be asked to verify your identity. Depending on the country in which you are creating the account, there are different options for verifying yourself, including using two-factor authentication or validating with a trusted device. Follow the on-screen instructions to complete the process.
7. Once successfully verified, it will create your Apple ID, and you can start downloading apps, music, and other content from iTunes or the App Store.

Now that you have an Apple ID, you can sign into iCloud and access all of Apple's cloud-based services on your MacBook Air or Pro.

Installing New Software

When it comes to downloading and installing new software for your MacBook Air or Pro, there are a few steps you'll need to follow. Here's an easy step-by-step guide for seniors to help make the process as simple as possible:

To begin with, you'll need to find the software you want to install. You can find most software through the App Store using a Mac or other online sources such as websites, download sites, and digital marketplaces. Make sure you read reviews and check to ensure the software is compatible with your MacBook before downloading.

Once you've located the appropriate software, choose the "Download" option. Depending on the size of the file you're downloading, this could take anywhere from a few seconds to a few minutes. Be sure to save the file in an easily-accessible location so you can find it later.

When the download is complete, locate and double-click on the software's installation file. It will open a window containing the installation instructions. Follow these instructions carefully to make sure everything is installed correctly.

When the installation process is complete, you may need to restart your computer to finish setting up the software. Depending on your security preferences, you may also be asked to enter an administrator password before completing the installation.

With the installation, you can start using your new software. Be sure to read any user manuals or guides with the software to get the best out of it.

Following these steps should give seniors an easy way to download and install new software on their MacBook Air or Pro.

Understanding and Using Apple's Pre-Installed Applications

Apple devices come pre-installed with various apps that you can use to complete multiple tasks. These apps provide seniors with many opportunities to stay connected, informed, and entertained. Here is a step-by-step guide on how to use some of these applications:

Message: This app that allows users to text back and forth with friends and family quickly. To use it, open the Messages app on your device, tap the "+" button in the upper right corner, and enter a phone number or email address to start a conversation.

Calendar: This handy app allows users to keep track of all their upcoming events in one place. To use it, open the Calendar app, create an event by tapping the "+" button in the upper right corner, and enter all necessary information.

Photos: Photos are a great way to store and share photos with friends and family. To use it, open the Photos app, tap the "+" button in the upper right corner, and select photos or videos to add to your library.

Safari: Safari is a web browser that allows you to access different websites on the internet. To use it, open the Safari app, type in a website address in the search bar at the top of the screen, and hit enter.

Maps: This app is a great way to find directions and explore the world around you. To use it, open the Maps app, type in your destination address in the search bar at the top of the screen, and hit enter.

By utilizing these apps on an Apple device, seniors can stay connected with their loved ones, be informed of important events, and explore the world around them. With its easy-to-use interface and helpful step-by-step guide, Apple devices are perfect for seniors new to technology.

Using the Navigation App

Navigation apps are an incredibly useful tool for seniors. With the help of these apps, seniors can easily find their way around unfamiliar locations and plan trips. They can also get important information about local attractions and services, making travel more enjoyable.

Using navigation apps on a MacBook is easy. Here's a step-by-step guide to getting you started:

Start by opening the App Store on your MacBook. Type in "navigation app" and browse through the options available. Once you find one that meets your needs, click "Get" or "Download" to install it onto your device.

Set up the app by inputting your basic information and preferences. It may include specifics such as your home address, favorite destinations, or any other details you'd like to save for quick access later.

Once the app is set up, locate the route you'd like to take. You can do this by searching for a specific address or simply entering your current location and the destination you'd like to reach. Once you input the details, the app will generate a route that is best suited for your needs.

Finally, follow the directions provided to make it to your destination safely and efficiently. Pay attention to the audio and visual cues given by the app, as they will provide important information about the route ahead.

Navigation apps can make it easier for seniors to explore new places and reach their destinations on time. Using them on a MacBook is easy, so why not try? With practice, you'll soon become a pro at using navigation apps!

Adjusting Display Settings

Keep a few things in mind when adjusting your MacBook Air or Pro. First and foremost, change the display settings for seniors. Seniors often have difficulty reading text on small screens, so adjusting the resolution and font size will help make it easier for them to read.

To adjust the resolution of your MacBook Air or Pro, open System Preferences from the dock or top Apple menu. Under Display in the System Preferences window, you can adjust the resolution to a lower level, making everything more visible for seniors.

To change the font size of your MacBook Air or Pro, select accessibility from the System Preferences window and then click on Display. You can then choose a larger font size that will make it easier for seniors to read.

Finally, adjust the brightness of your MacBook Air or Pro so that it is not too bright or too dim. You can do it the same way as changing the resolution and font size. Once you have adjusted these settings for seniors, your MacBook Air or Pro should be much easier to use.

Adding Wallpaper and Personalizing the Look of Your MacBook

Once you've selected a wallpaper, it's time to personalize your MacBook Air or Pro. You can customize the look of your laptop by changing its desktop background and adding personal icons and folders.

Choose an image from your computer library or the web for your desired background. If you plan to use an image from the web, ensure you have the right to use it. Then, choose System Preferences and select Desktop & Screen Saver. Click on Choose Folder and select your preferred wallpaper.

Tips:

For easy access to your custom background, you can also click and drag the image file onto your desktop once you've selected a wallpaper. Spice up your MacBook Air or Pro by adding personal icons and folders.

Managing Files & Applications

Organizing your files and applications on your MacBook Air or Pro is the first step in managing them. It's essential to ensure all your files, folders, and documents are in an easy-to-find spot.

You can organize them by type, such as all of your photos or music in one folder, or by date. You can also use labels and tags to help organize your files and make them easier to find.

Organizing files and applications on your MacBook Air or Pro can seem daunting, but it doesn't have to be. Following these simple steps, you can keep your MacBook organized and running smoothly.

Creating Folders

Another way to keep your MacBook organized is to create a folder for each application you use. It will help keep all the associated files in one place, making it easier to find what you need. You can also use the Finder window to search for files and folders on your Mac quickly.

Data Back-Up

Finally, once you've organized your files and applications, it's important to back them up regularly. You can use the Time Machine feature on your Mac to create a backup of all your data. It will protect you if something happens and you lose your files. You can also create an online data backup with a cloud storage service like iCloud or Dropbox.

Customization

Once you are familiar with the basics of managing files and applications on your MacBook Air or Pro, there are many ways to customize your MacBook to suit your needs.

You can change how your MacBook looks by personalizing its wallpaper, dock, and menu bar.

You can also alter the system's display settings to make your fonts easier to read or change the colors of icons and windows.

Understanding the Basic Function

When managing files and folders on your MacBook Air or Pro, it's important to understand the basic functions each device offers. You can organize your files and folders in several ways, including sorting them into categories or creating a hierarchical structure.

Performing Different Functions

Once you have a good idea of organizing your files, the following steps will guide you through managing your files and folders on your MacBook Air or Pro.

- Open Finder and select the folder you want to manage. You can also open Finder by clicking the magnifying glass icon at the top right of your screen.

- Select a **view mode**, such as list, icon, or column view, to help you organize your files and folders. You can customize the view mode by clicking the "View" menu at the top of the screen.

- Once your files are sorted into categories, create subfolders for categorizing them further. To create a folder, click on the file in the Finder menu and select "New Folder."

- **Rename** folders and files by double-clicking on their name and typing in the new name.

- **Move** your files and folders to different locations within the same folder or across other folders using drag-and-drop. To move multiple items simultaneously, use Command + click or Shift + click to select the files, then drag and drop them into their new location.

- To **delete** a file or folder, right-click on it and select "Move to Trash." You can also empty the trash by selecting "Empty Trash" in the Finder menu.

- To **search** for a particular file or folder, use the Finder search box at the top right corner of your screen. Enter the name of the file or folder you're looking for and hit "Enter" to begin your search.

- To **share** a file or folder, right-click on it and select "Share." You can then choose how to share it with others via email, AirDrop, or a cloud service.

- If you want to **back up** your files and folders, use the Time Machine utility with your MacBook Air or Pro. To access this feature, go to System Preferences and select the Time Machine icon. Follow the instructions to set up a daily backup schedule for your files.

Following these steps will help you effectively manage your files and folders on your MacBook Air or Pro. With a bit of patience and practice, you can master the art of file organization in no time!

CHAPTER 8: SETTING UP AND
USING AN EMAIL ACCOUNT

You can easily send and receive emails to other users when you have an email account on your MacBook Air or Pro. Setting up your email is important so you only get some important messages. Here is a step-by-step guide for setting up and managing an email account on your MacBook Air or Pro:

1. Open the **Mail App**. You can find this app in your Applications folder or by searching for it in Spotlight Search, which is located at the top right of your screen.

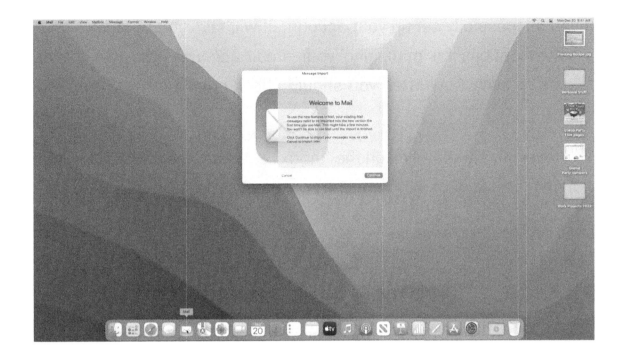

2. Click on the "**Add Account**" option in the window's bottom left corner. It will bring up a dialogue box asking you to enter your email address and password.

3. Enter your email address and password into the appropriate fields, then select the type of account you want to use (e.g., Gmail, Yahoo!, etc.). Then click "Sign In."

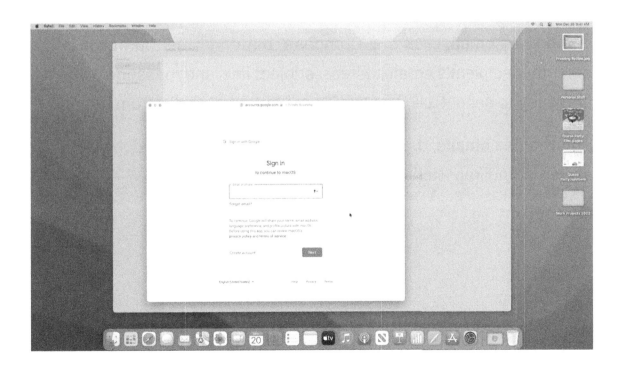

4. If you successfully set up your account, it will take you to a new window with a list of options for managing your email account. You can decide which folders to sync, how often you should check emails for new messages, and more.

5. To **view your emails**, click on the "Inbox" button at the top of the window. You will then see a list of all your incoming emails.

1. To **send an email**, click the "Compose" button at the top of the window and enter the recipient's email address, subject line, and message body. When you are ready to send it, click on the "Send" button at the bottom right corner.

2. To **organize emails**, drag them into folders in the left sidebar. It will make it easier to find important messages when needed.

Sending and Receiving Emails

When sending emails, it's important to remember to be thoughtful and courteous. After all, email is a form of communication that many people rely on. Follow these steps to ensure your emails are sent correctly:

1. Open the Mail app on your MacBook Air. You can find this by clicking the "Launchpad" icon on your dock and selecting the "Mail" app.

2. Select the "Compose" button to create a new message.

3. Enter your recipient's email address in the "To:" field, and fill out any other relevant fields (like subject or cc) if desired.

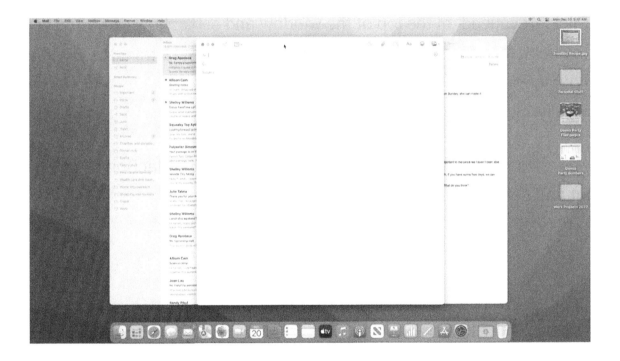

4. Write your message in the body of the email. Double-check any spelling or grammar mistakes, and then attach any files if necessary.

5. Once you're finished, click "Send" in the upper right corner. It will send your message off to its recipient!

Customizing Your Inbox

Once you have set up your email account, it is time to begin customizing your inbox. You can do it in a few simple steps:

1. Select the "Mail" tab from the top of the screen and then click on "Preferences."
2. It will now direct you to a new menu where you can choose the type of account you want to use. You can select either an IMAP or a POP for your email account.
3. Once you have selected a type of account, click "Accounts" at the top of the window and choose your email address from the list on the left-hand side.
4. In the Account Information section, you can customize your preferences. Here you can set the font size for your emails and configure whether or not you want to receive messages from blocked senders.
5. Click "Advanced" at the top of the window and select how often you want mail to check for new mail. You can choose from every 15 minutes, 30 minutes, 1 hour, or manually.
6. Finally, click "Save" to apply your changes.

Following these steps, you can customize your inbox in MacBook Air for a more efficient and personalized mail experience.

CHAPTER 9: ADJUSTING
YOUR SYSTEM PREFERENCES

The System Preferences feature in the MacBook Air or Pro can adjust settings and customize your laptop's operation. To access this feature, click on the Apple menu at the top of your screen and select "System Preferences." The various categories available in System Preferences include Personal, Hardware, Internet & Wireless, Security & Privacy, and App Store & Software Update.

Personal

This category allows you to customize settings related to your user account, including setting up the appearance of the Dock and desktop. You can also adjust login and display options and change the default web browser.

Hardware

This category contains settings related to your laptop's hardware, such as sound, displays, printers and scanners, keyboard shortcuts, and a trackpad. You can also adjust the energy saver settings that determine how much power your laptop consumes when not in use.

Internet and Wireless

This category allows you to configure your internet and wireless connection settings, including Wi-Fi networks and Bluetooth devices. You can also set up a virtual private network (VPN) connection if needed.

Security & Privacy

This category contains settings related to the security of your laptop, including the Firewall feature, which blocks incoming connections. You can also adjust the settings for File Vault, which will encrypt your hard drive and protect it from unauthorized access.

App Store & Software Update

This category provides settings related to the App Store and software updates, allowing you to control when updates are downloaded and installed. You can also set up automatic app downloads if you wish. By adjusting the settings in System Preferences, you can customize how your MacBook Air or Pro operates and make it easier to use. Be sure to take some time to review each category and adjust the settings as needed.

Customizing Your MacBook

Launchpad

Once you have clicked on the Launchpad icon and your home page is open, it will present you with a grid of icons representing the applications installed on your computer. You can move these around to customize your Home Screen's layout in any way you want. To do this, click and drag one icon onto another until they appear alongside each other.

If you want to delete an application or folder from your Launchpad home screen, you must press and hold down on the icon for about two seconds until it begins to jiggle. You'll then see a small 'x' icon appear in the top left-hand corner of the icon, which you can use to delete from your Launchpad page.

You can also organize your applications into folders on your Launchpad home screen. To do this, click and drag one application icon onto another until they appear alongside each other. It will prompt you with the option to 'Create Folder,' in which you can name anything you want. Once you have done this, click on the folder's icon, which will open to display all the applications.

Dock

The Dock is a great way to keep the apps you use most readily accessible on your MacBook Air

or Pro. It's easy to customize, so you can ensure it works for your workflow.

To get started, open up System Preferences and select "Dock" from the list of options. Then, you'll be presented with several options to customize the look and feel of your Dock.

You can adjust the size of your Dock by using the slider at the bottom of the window. It enables you to make it larger or smaller depending on how much screen real estate you want to dedicate to displaying apps in the Dock.

To customize the position of your Dock, you can use either of the options in the Position on Screen section. You can choose to have it positioned on your screen's left or right side, depending on which is more comfortable for you.

If you want to display only certain apps in the Dock, you can use the Automatically Hide and Show the Dock option. This way, only those apps you select will be visible in the Dock any time.

Desktop

Open the System Preferences window to customize your MacBook Air or Pro's desktop. You can change several settings, such as color and wallpaper, fonts, sounds, and power options.

Change the background of your desktop by clicking on the Desktop & Screen Saver option from the System Preferences window.

You can choose from the pre-installed wallpapers or import your images as wallpaper by selecting the Desktop and Screen Saver icons.

To change the font of the text on your desktop, select the "Fonts" option from System Preferences. You can also toggle between different fonts if you wish to make changes at a later time.

Choose the sound preferences for your MacBook Air or Pro's desktop by selecting the "Sound" option from System Preferences. You can customize the sound settings for alerts, system sounds, and more.

Select the "Energy Saver" option from the System Preferences window to conserve battery power and reduce unnecessary background applications. It will allow you to set preferences for when your computer should go into sleep mode, when it should dim its screen, and more.

To configure security settings such as password protection and file encryption, select the "Security & Privacy" option from System Preferences. Here you can set up a secure password and choose which files you want to keep encrypted.

Finally, if you want to customize your MacBook Air or Pro's desktop further, select the "Accessibility" option from System Preferences. Here you can change settings for magnification, visual effects, and more.

Following these steps, you can easily customize your MacBook Air or Pro's desktop to suit your needs and preferences.

The best part about customizing your MacBook Air or Pro's desktop is that all these settings are simple to change at any time. If you need to make changes, open the System Preferences window and adjust your settings as required. It makes it easy to keep your MacBook looking great, no matter what changes you may make over time.

Menus

Once you've finished customizing the dock and desktop, it's time to move on to the menus. You can customize the MacBook Air or Pro's menus by following simple steps.

First, open System Preferences from your dock and select Keyboard & Mouse. Select the Keyboard Shortcuts tab in this menu. To customize the menu, choose the menus you want to change and press the + sign.

Once you've chosen your shortcuts, click "OK." Your customizations will now be active once you close the menu. If you want to delete a shortcut, select it in the Keyboard Shortcuts tab and click the - sign.

You can also customize menus from individual applications. To do this, open the application's preferences and look for the "Keyboard" or "Shortcuts" section. Here, you can set custom shortcuts for menus or individual commands in the menu.

Customizing both system and application menus is a great way to increase your MacBook Air or Pro productivity. You can customize the menus with just a few clicks to make them work best for you.

CHAPTER 10: SETTING UP THE INTERNET

f you want a wireless connection, you will need access to a Wi-Fi network. It could be a public Wi-Fi hotspot or a private home network. Setting up Wi-Fi on your MacBook can be confusing, especially for seniors who could be more tech-savvy. This guide will walk you through the steps of setting up your Wi-Fi connection on your MacBook to help make it as easy and stress-free as possible.

- First, open the System Preferences window. You can do this by clicking on the Apple icon in your menu and selecting System Preferences.

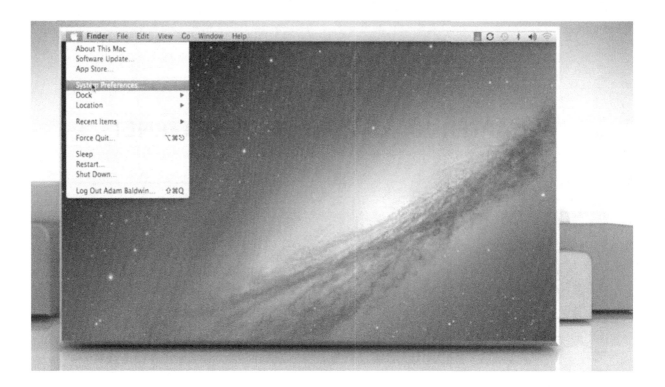

- Once you open the System Preferences window, click on the Network tab. It should be located at the top of the window. Then select Wi-Fi from the list of network options that appears.

- Next, select your Wi-Fi network from the list of available networks. If you don't see your network listed, click on "Other..." and enter the name of your Wi-Fi network in the box that appears. You may also be asked for a password if your network is secure.

- Once you select your Wi-Fi network, you should see the status of the connection change to "Connected." If it still says "Disconnected," double-check that you entered the correct network name and password if needed.

Your MacBook is now connected to your Wi-Fi network! Try loading a web page or two in your browser to verify that everything is working correctly. If you can access the internet without any issues, then your Wi-Fi setup is complete.

Wired Connection Setup

To complete the setup of a wired connection for your MacBook, you will need the following items: an Ethernet cable, an active internet connection, and your MacBook.

Step 1: Connect one end of the Ethernet cable to the back of your active router.

Step 2: Connect the other end of the Ethernet cable to your MacBook.

Step 3: Ensure the Ethernet cable is securely connected to your router and MacBook.

Step 4: Open up System Preferences on your MacBook.

Step 5: Select "Network" from the list of icons in the System Preferences window.

Step 6: On the Network page, select "Ethernet" from the list of connection types.

Step 7: The Ethernet status will change to "connected" once the laptop has successfully established an internet connection with your router.

Configuring Network Settings

This guide will provide seniors with step-by-step instructions for setting up their MacBook Air or Pro so they can connect to the internet as quickly and efficiently as possible.

The first step is to connect your MacBook Air or Pro to a Wi-Fi network. To do this, click on the Wi-Fi icon at the top of the screen near the battery indicator. Select your desired network from the list. If prompted for a password, be sure to enter it correctly.

The next step is to configure your DNS settings. To do this, open System Preferences and click on the Network icon. Then, select Wi-Fi from the list of interfaces at the left side of the window and click Advanced in the bottom right corner of the screen.

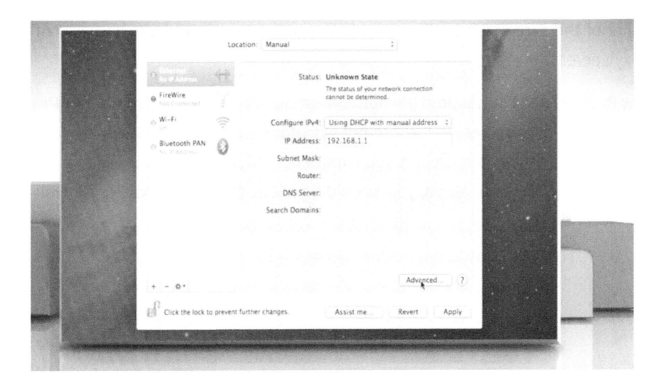

Under DNS, click + and enter the IP addresses of your preferred DNS servers.

Finally, you must set up a proxy server if you use one. To do this, open System Preferences and click on the Network icon again. Select Wi-Fi from the list of interfaces at the left side of the window and click Advanced in the bottom right corner of the screen. Under Proxies, click + and enter the address and port of your proxy server.

Now that you have configured the network settings on your MacBook Air or Pro, you should be able to connect to the internet with no trouble. Double-check your settings to ensure everything is correct if you experience difficulty getting online or loading web pages. With these steps, you should be ready to start browsing the web with your new device!

CHAPTER 11: USING YOUR MACBOOK
AIR AND PRO'S APPS

The MacBook Air and Pro have several built-in apps designed to help you stay productive and connected. This step-by-step guide will teach you how to use the most popular apps to make the most of your MacBook Air or Pro.

Safari

Safari is Apple's web browser and is the best way to browse the internet on your MacBook Air or Pro. To open Safari, click on the blue compass icon in your dock. You can enter a web address into the URL bar at the top to go directly to a specific website. You can also search the web by entering your search term in the same bar. Safari can also store links to your favorite websites, so you don't have to type in the URL every time.

To start with Safari, open the app by clicking the Safari icon in your dock.

- In the top left corner, you'll see a search bar where you type in the website address, you'd like to visit. To the right of the search bar, you'll see several buttons that allow you to customize your browsing experience.

- The back and forward buttons allow you to move between web pages you've already visited. The refresh button will reload the page you're currently viewing. The Safari menu allows you to customize your settings and manage your bookmarks, history, and more.

- The next section of the Safari window contains tabs. Each tab allows you to view a different webpage, so if you're researching multiple topics at once, this is the perfect feature. To open a new tab, click the plus sign in the upper right corner of your Safari window.

- At the bottom of the Safari window, you'll find your favorite bar. It is where you can keep track of all your favorite sites that you visit often. To add a website to your favorites bar, click the star icon next to the web address.

- You can also customize your browsing experience by downloading extensions or plugins. Extensions are small software that adds extra features to your browser and makes it easier to use.

Finally, you can customize your security settings in Safari by opening the Preferences window. Here you can choose which type of websites to allow and how much information about you to share.

Now that you're familiar with the basics of Safari, you can start exploring the internet! Whether researching a topic or finding something new, Safari is the perfect tool to help you find what you need.

Calendar

The Calendar app helps you keep track of events, appointments, and more. Click on the blue icon with a calendar picture in your dock to open it. To add an event, click on the + button in the top right corner and enter the details of your event. You can also sync your calendar with other devices, such as an iPhone or iPad, to access it wherever you go.

Keeping Track of Schedules, Appointments, and Reminders with Calendar

For elders, a calendar app is a perfect tool for remembering and scheduling events, appointments, and reminders. The first step in using the calendar app on your MacBook Air or Pro is to open it. To do this, go to Finder from the dock and select "Applications" from the left-hand menu. From there, you will find the Calendar located under "iLife." Click on the app, and it will open and take up the full screen of your MacBook Air or Pro.

Once you have opened the Calendar, you will see a basic view with only a few categories on the left-hand side. These include "Events," which is where you can add new events, "Reminders," where you can add reminders to yourself for upcoming tasks or appointments; and "Calendars." You can view your calendars from other sources like Google Calendar or iCloud.

From here, you can add new events for any appointment or a reminder you need to remember. To add an event, click on the "+" sign at the top right corner of the Calendar app. You will then be given a form to fill out with information such as date, time, duration, location, and description. Once you have filled this out, click "Create," and your new event is saved.

Click on the "Reminders" section in the left-hand panel to add a reminder. Here you will see the option to create a new reminder with similar fields as when creating an event. Once you have filled out the form, click "Create," and your new reminder is saved.

You can also add calendars from other sources, such as Google Calendar or iCloud. To do this, click "Calendars" in the left-hand panel and select "Add Account."

Here you will be given a choice to add either a Google account or an iCloud account. Once you have added your desired accounts, you can view all of your calendars in one place on the MacBook Air or Pro.

With the Calendar app, you have all the tools necessary to manage any appointment, event, or reminder with ease. Now that you know how to use it, you can feel confident knowing that your scheduled events and reminders are always at your fingertips.

You can easily become an expert at managing your Calendar on your MacBook Air or Pro with a little practice.

Mail

The Mail app is a great way to keep up with your email. Click on the blue icon with an envelope in your dock to open it. You can log into your email accounts and view, send and receive messages. You can also add multiple email accounts, so you don't have to switch between them.

Photos

The Photos app is the perfect way to view, organize and share photos on your MacBook Air or Pro. To open it, click on the orange icon with a picture of a flower in your dock. You can upload photos from your computer or other devices and view them in the app. You can also edit pictures with basic tools such as cropping and color adjustment or use more advanced features such as retouching and filters.

Notes

Notes is a great way to take quick notes, organize ideas or create simple lists on your MacBook Air or Pro. To open it, click on the yellow icon with a picture of a notepad in your dock. You can also add checklists, add images and create folders to help keep your notes organized.

App Store Applications

The App Store on your MacBook Air and Pro is a great source to find apps that can help you get the most out of your technology. Whether it's managing finances, staying entertained, or communicating with family, plenty of apps are available for seniors over 65 to enhance their lives.

To access the App Store, open the Finder window and select "Applications." From there, you will see an icon with a blue background titled "App Store." Once that is opened, you can search for applications such as word processing programs or finance management software.

When you find an app that interests you, click on it, and it will take you to a page with a description and user reviews. Once you decide it's the app for you, click "Get" to download it for free or "Buy" if a fee is associated.

Once the app is on your MacBook Air or Pro, you can access it by clicking the Launchpad icon in your Dock bar. You can also search for the app name in the Spotlight search bar or find it directly in the Finder window.

The App Store offers a great selection of apps for seniors that can help make your life easier and more enjoyable. Explore all that it has to offer to find the apps that work best for you.

With a few simple steps, you can access and utilize all the great applications available in the App Store on your MacBook Air or Pro! Enjoy exploring and finding new ways to stay connected and entertained.

iCloud Services & Settings

Seniors looking to take advantage of iCloud services and settings on their MacBook Air or Pro laptops can do so easily with the help of Apple's built-in apps. These apps allow users to store files, photos, contacts, and more in the cloud and access them from any device.

The most commonly used app for iCloud services is iCloud Drive, which provides users easy access to their stored files. The Photos app allows seniors to easily store and organize photos and share them with friends and family.

Contacts can also be kept in the cloud via the Contacts app, making it easier for seniors to stay connected with others. Finally, music can be managed through iTunes so that seniors can listen to their favorite tunes on any device. With these iCloud services and settings, MacBook Air and Pro laptops are a great choice for seniors who want to stay connected with friends and family members while also having access to their most important files.

For an even more convenient experience, you can integrate many apps into the menu bar on the MacBook. It allows seniors to quickly access their iCloud services and settings with just a few clicks. Additionally, numerous third-party apps can help streamline the process of managing photos, contacts, music, and other files.

MacBook Air and Pro laptops offer seniors an easy way to stay connected and take advantage of iCloud services. With the help of Apple's built-in apps and third-party applications, seniors can easily manage their files and stay connected with friends and family members.

These laptops are also great for keeping in touch with the latest news, trends, sports scores, and other information. The web browsers included in MacBook Air and Pro models provide seniors with a fast and secure way to browse the internet. Additionally, Apple's built-in apps like News and Safari can help keep seniors up-to-date on what's happening around them.

MacBook Air and Pro models offer seniors an easy way to stay connected with friends, family, and the world around them while also taking advantage of iCloud services. With their built-in apps and third-party applications, seniors can easily manage their files, stay up-to-date on the latest news, and video chat with loved ones from wherever they are.

By taking advantage of these features, MacBook Air and Pro laptops can be an excellent choice for seniors who want to stay connected and get the most out of their devices.

iWork Suite of Word Processing, Presentation, and Spreadsheet Apps

iWork Suite of Word Processing MacBook Air and Pro's Apps is an intuitive, user-friendly set of word-processing applications designed specifically for seniors. All apps are designed with the needs of seniors in mind, making them simple to use and understand. They can easily create and share documents with others with a few clicks. iWork Suite is also compatible with other popular word processing applications like Microsoft Word and Google Docs, so it's easy to switch between different formats. With iWork Suite, seniors can stay connected and productive no matter where they are.

iWork Suite is also packed with the following features that make it perfect for seniors.

Vision Impairments Features

Its Voice Over feature allows users to navigate through the apps with voice commands. Also, its Magnifier tool makes text and images easier to read— both of which are helpful for those with vision impairments. It also has an Accessibility Inspector that makes it much easier to identify and fix any issues with the document, such as font size or color contrast. Finally, iWork Suite is designed to be familiar, so seniors can easily pick up and use the apps without extensive training.

These applications make it easy for seniors to create documents, spreadsheets, and presentations on their MacBook Air or Pro in simple steps.

Word-Processing Application

Pages is an intuitive word-processing application that creates everything from letters to brochures. It offers many options for creating a new document, including templates and custom page sizes, orientation, and margins. Moreover, you can make text stand out is easy with the font selection tools, which allow you to choose from various fonts and styles such as bold, italic, and underline.

Pages have various formatting tools that allow you to make text bigger or smaller, change line spacing and indentation, add bullets or numbered lists, and more.

Seniors looking for word processing software that's user-friendly and easy to understand need look no further than iWork Suite of Word Processing MacBook Air and Pro's Apps. It provides a powerful suite of word-processing tools designed specifically for their needs, making it simple and convenient to stay connected and effective on the go. With iWork Suite of Word Processing MacBook Air and Pro's Apps, staying connected and productive anywhere has never been easier!

Creating Presentations

Keynote is an application that makes creating presentations on the MacBook Air or Pro easy and fun. It allows seniors to quickly create slides with text, photos and graphics. Seniors can add titles, subtitles, and body text to each slide and insert images and shapes. You can also add animations to slides to make them more engaging and dynamic.

The iWork suite of apps makes it easy for seniors to create paper records, spreadsheets, and demonstrations on their MacBook Air or Pro in a few simple steps. From setting up documents to adding text and graphics to animating presentations, the iWork suite offers powerful tools that allow seniors to express their creativity.

You can become an expert in no time with a little practice and exploration! If you're ready to take your skills to the next level, consider taking an online or in-person class to learn more about the iWork Suite of apps.

Spreadsheet Apps

The MacBook Air and Pro are both great options for seniors looking for a versatile computer with plenty of features. Spreadsheet apps make data entry and analysis easier for everyone, especially those new to computers or unfamiliar with more sophisticated software solutions.

For the MacBook Air, Numbers is an excellent option - it's pre-installed, user-friendly, and feature-rich. Numbers support data entry with tables, graphs, mathematical equations, and labeling of columns and rows - all designed to make the process as intuitive and straightforward as possible. It also has a great set of features for analyzing data, such as sorting, filtering, and automatic calculations. With Numbers' powerful features, seniors can quickly and easily create and edit spreadsheets, allowing them to quickly draw valuable insights and make informed decisions.

The MacBook Pro also comes with a great spreadsheet app - Microsoft Excel. Excel is the industry standard for data analysis. It offers an impressive range of tools and features that allow users to do everything from basic calculations to more advanced statistical analysis. It's also pre-installed, making it easy for seniors to get up and running with the app without going through a lengthy installation process.

Excel is incredibly powerful thanks to features like pivot tables, VBA (Visual Basic for Applications) support, and advanced graphing capabilities. All these help users create sophisticated visual presentations of their data.

MacBook Air and Pro are great for seniors, offering an easy-to-use spreadsheet app that simplifies data entry and analysis. With either option, seniors can take advantage of powerful features to draw insights from their data and make informed decisions.

iMovie and GarageBand for Audio/Video Editing and Production

For seniors interested in exploring audio/video editing and production, Apple's iMovie and GarageBand are great tools, to begin with. Both programs are available on the MacBook Air and Pro models. They offer many features for creating high-quality videos and music. With iMovie, users can quickly produce movies with professional transitions, titles, and effects. GarageBand allows users to record, edit and mix their music with over 200 instruments, loops, and sound effects.

iMovie and GarageBand provide a variety of tutorials for different levels of experience, so seniors can learn the basics or dive deeper into more advanced techniques. Additionally, both programs are intuitively designed with an easy-to-use interface that seniors can understand quickly. With iMovie and GarageBand, creating videos and music has always been challenging for seniors.

Users also have access to a library of stock footage, photos, and sound effects – allowing users to create more complex projects with ease. Furthermore, both programs allow users to easily share their creations, either via email, messaging services, or directly to social media.

For seniors looking to get started with audio/video editing and production on their MacBook Air or Pro, iMovie and GarageBand are excellent programs to begin exploring the world of multimedia creation. With these tools, seniors can easily create videos and music they can be proud of.

Additionally, Apple offers free online courses and video tutorials to help users get started quickly. There are paid professional classes and workshops available for more in-depth instruction for seniors who want to improve their skills. With the proper guidance and resources, seniors can unlock the power of iMovie and GarageBand and start creating professional-level projects in no time. So, don't hesitate to explore the audio/video editing and production world with Apple's fantastic tools!

iTunes and Apple Music for Consuming Media

Apple Music and iTunes are two of the most popular digital media stores for senior citizens. With iTunes, seniors can purchase movies, music, tv shows, audiobooks, and podcasts with just one click. Apple Music offers access to over 50 million songs in its library--all available for streaming or download. It also includes exclusive playlists curated by industry professionals and the ability to create and share your playlists.

The MacBook Air and Pro are excellent devices for seniors who want to enjoy their digital media library. With their high-quality Retina display, powerful processor, and long battery life, these laptops are great for streaming music, watching movies, or playing games on the go. And with iCloud integration, seniors can sync their Apple Music library across all devices. So, whether at home or on the go, they can always access and enjoy their favorite tunes.

With iTunes and Apple Music, seniors have a convenient way to consume digital media on their MacBook Air and Pro. And with the right setup, they can easily organize, enrich and share their media library with family and friends. So, if you're looking for a way to keep your music library organized and up-to-date, look no further than iTunes and Apple Music on the MacBook Air and Pro.

Step 1: Download iTunes from the App Store on your MacBook Air and Pro.

Step 2: Once downloaded, open the program and log into your Apple ID account.

Step 3: At the top of the screen, select "Music" to begin streaming or purchasing music.

Step 4: Browse the music library and add songs to your playlist.

Step 5: Click on the desired song or album price to purchase music. You will be prompted to enter your Apple ID account password to confirm the purchase.

Step 6: iTunes will download them directly into your library after making purchases. You can access this by clicking on the "library" tab from the top of the iTunes window.

Step 7: To access Apple Music, click on the "For You" option at the top of the screen.

Step 8: Select your favorite genres of music and begin streaming songs or entire albums with a free three-month trial.

Step 9: To purchase music, follow the steps outlined in Step 5.

Step 10: Enjoy your personalized library of media!

Following these simple steps, you can easily use iTunes and Apple Music on your MacBook Air or Pro to consume your favorite media!

Social Networking & Video Chat Apps

Seniors can easily stay connected with family, friends, and even medical professionals through social networking and video chat apps on their MacBook Air or Pro. Apple's built-in FaceTime app is a great way for seniors to connect face-to-face with loved ones who are not near them. Some third-party apps, such as Skype, Zoom, and Google Hangouts, offer video chat capabilities. These apps can be downloaded for free in the Mac App Store and used on any recent MacBook Air or Pro model.

Social networking, a great way to stay connected with loved ones while having fun, is also available to seniors on their MacBook Air or Pro. Popular social media apps such as Facebook, you can download Instagram and Twitter for free in the Mac App Store. Additionally, various third-party apps available to seniors can help them stay connected with family and friends.

Seniors can also benefit from using their MacBook Air or Pro to access important medical information. Many healthcare providers offer online portals for their patients, which allow them to access medical records, review lab results securely, and pay bills online. You can access these portals through the web browser on any recent MacBook Air or Pro model.

By utilizing these modern technology tools, seniors can easily stay connected with family, friends, and medical professionals. Whether it's a video chat session with far-away family members or accessing medical records, seniors can use their MacBook Air or Pro to make life easier and stay connected.

Connecting to Social Media Platforms

With social networking apps, video chat capabilities, and other helpful tools available on the MacBook Air or Pro, seniors can stay connected easily. With just a few clicks of their Apple device, they can easily remain involved in the lives of those they love and access important medical information when needed. Ultimately, these modern tools provide an easy way for seniors to stay connected and active in our rapidly changing world.

When it comes to connecting to social media platforms with your MacBook, it's quite easy once you know how. There are four main steps to get started:

1. Register for an account on your chosen platform, like Facebook, Twitter, or Instagram. You can do this easily from your MacBook Air or Pro by visiting the website of your chosen platform and signing up for an account.

2. Once registered for the account, you can download the app on your laptop if available. All major social media platforms offer a free app for easy access to the platform.

3. Log in to the app or website with the account details you created during registration and explore its features. You can start by customizing your profile, adding friends, writing posts, and engaging with other users on the platform.

4. Once familiar with the basics, you can explore more advanced features like creating groups, following news sources, or setting up notifications. Your account is safe and secure with the right settings and security measures.

These four simple steps are all it takes to get started using social media platforms on your MacBook Air or Pro. So, what are you waiting for? Get connected and start enjoying the world of social media!

By utilizing the helpful and user-friendly features of their MacBook Air or Pro, seniors can remain active in their communities and connected with those they love most. Social networking apps allow them to share photos and stories. In contrast, video chat apps provide a convenient way to see each other face-to-face. With the help of their Apple device, seniors can stay informed, connected, and engaged.

Sending Files Through AirDrop

The AirDrop feature makes it easy to share photos, videos, documents, or other files with the people nearby you.

When using the AirDrop feature on MacBook Air or Pro, here are the steps to follow:

1. Make sure that your device is discoverable by switching on Bluetooth and Wi-Fi from the menu bar.
2. Select the file you would like to share with another device using the Finder window or any other program which supports drag & drop.
3. Click on the AirDrop icon to bring up a list of devices you can share your file with, or drag and drop it onto a user's name in Finder.
4. Depending on the type of device you're sending the files to, they will have to accept or decline the transfer through a pop-up on their device.
5. When the transfer is accepted, it will send the file over, and you can check in the Finder window to see when it's done.
6. Once complete, an alert will appear, mentioning that the other user has successfully received the files.

You can now disconnect your Bluetooth and Wi-Fi connection to optimize your battery life.

Following these steps, you can easily share files with other Apple devices using AirDrop. It's fast and easy, so give it a try!

However, if you are having issues using AirDrop, some troubleshooting tips can help.

When using AirDrop, ensure the sender and receiver have Wi-Fi and Bluetooth turned on. Also, check to be sure that you are within about 30 feet of each other so that the devices can detect one another. If you still can't connect after making sure these settings are correct, try restarting both devices and then try connecting again.

If you still have trouble connecting, check the versions of iOS or macOS that your devices are running. AirDrop works best when both devices use the most recent operating system version.

CHAPTER 12: MANAGING
PHOTOS AND MUSIC

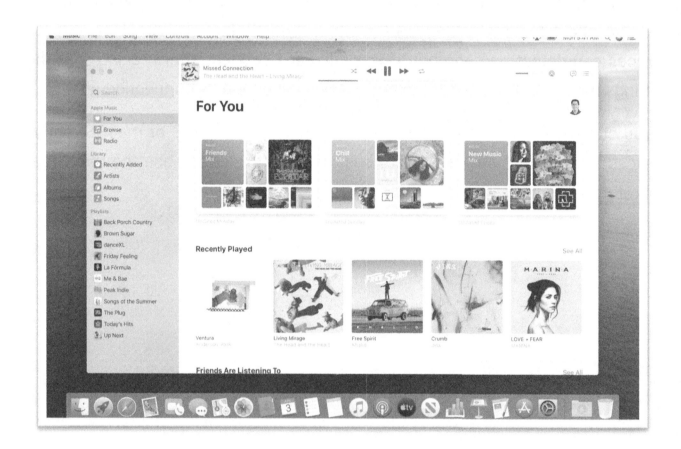

The MacBook Air or Pro allows seniors to easily manage their photos and music. With a few clicks, they can manage their photo library, create new albums, and transfer images to other devices. They can also organize and play their music with the iTunes player.

Organizing Photos: The Photos app on the Mac makes it easy to organize and manage photos. Senior users can create and rename albums, add pictures to albums, delete photos, or move them to different albums. They can also transfer images from the Mac to other devices or import images from external media sources.

Playing Music: The iTunes app on a Mac provides many features for playing music. Seniors can choose from different audio formats, create playlists, and even burn music to CDs or DVDs. They can access their iTunes library using the Apple Music service on other devices, such as an iPhone or iPod.

Overall, managing photos and music with a Mac is easy. With just a few clicks of the mouse, seniors can quickly and easily organize their photo library, transfer images, create playlists, and burn CDs.

Managing photos and music has always been challenging with Mac's intuitive interface.

Making Backup Copies: To ensure that all of their photos and music remain safe, seniors should back up their files regularly. Macs provide various backup options, including iCloud and local storage devices such as external hard drives. By backing up their files in multiple locations, seniors can ensure that their photos and music are always available if something happens to the original copies.

Finding New Music: The iTunes app provides access to hundreds of thousands of songs, albums, and music videos. Seniors can browse through different genres and artists to find new music or use the Genius feature to get recommendations based on their current library.

The Mac's intuitive interface allows seniors to manage their photos and music easily. With just a few clicks, they can organize their photo library, transfer images to other devices, create playlists and even find new music. By backing up their files in multiple locations, they can also ensure that their photos and music remain safe for years.

Editing Photos with Photos & Albums

The Photos & Albums feature on a MacBook Air, or Pro, is one of the best ways to organize and edit digital photos. With this guide, seniors can learn how to edit their pictures in just a few simple steps.

Step 1: Open Your Photos & Albums App

To begin, open the Photos & Albums app on your MacBook Air or Pro. You can find the app icon in the dock at the bottom of your screen.

Step 2: Select a Photo to Edit

Once the Photos & Albums app is open, you will see a list of all your albums and photos stored on your computer. To select an image to edit, click on the desired album and choose the photo you want to edit by clicking it once.

Step 3: Edit Your Photo

Now that you have selected your photo, you can start editing! To do this, use the tools located at the top of the window. These are divided into four categories: Edit, Enhance, Filter, and Adjust.

The *Edit tab* contains cropping, straightening, rotating, flipping, and more tools. To use any of these options, select the action you want to take from the list of available edits in the drop-down menu.

The *Enhance tab* contains a single button for auto-enhancement. This tool automatically adjusts color and contrast for a better-looking photo.

The *Filters tab* offers pre-made filters for your photos, such as Black & White or Sepia. You can also create your custom filters using the sliders.

Finally, the *Adjust tab* contains tools for adjusting your photos' tone, color, and brightness.

Step 4: Save Your Photo

Once you are happy with the edits you have made to your photo, click the "Save" button in the upper right-hand corner. You can also export your image as a jpeg or file type.

And that's it! Now you know how to edit photos with Photos & Albums on your MacBook Air or Pro. You can quickly turn any image into a masterpiece with just a few simple steps.

Taking Notes & Recording Audio with Voice Memos

You must connect an external microphone before recording if you have a MacBook Pro. Plug the microphone into your MacBook's audio input jack, then select it from the 'Input' menu in your Sound preferences. You can also adjust the sensitivity and other settings for your microphone there.

The built-in microphone should be ready to use if you have a MacBook Air. There is an 'Input' tab in your Sound preferences where you can adjust your microphone's sensitivity and other settings.

Recording with Voice Memos

Once your audio recording setup is complete, launch the Voice Memos app on your MacBook. Click the red 'Record' button to begin recording, and use the tools at the bottom of the window to adjust settings such as recording quality and playback speed.

When you are finished recording, click the blue 'Stop' button. It will save your voice memo in your Audio folder.

Taking Notes While Recording Voice Memos

Taking notes while recording voice memos can be invaluable for remembering important ideas and details. You can use the Notes app on your MacBook to take notes while recording without interrupting the flow of the conversation.

Launch the Notes app, create a new note, and start typing. Suppose you pause the recording and press 'cmd+shift+3' on your keyboard. It will temporarily pause your recording while you take notes. When you're finished taking notes, press 'cmd+shift+3' again to resume the recording.

Sharing Your Voice Memos

Once you have finished recording, you can share your voice memos with others by exporting them from the Voice Memos app. Select the voice memo from the list and click the 'Share' button in the window's top right corner. You'll be able to select which format you'd like to export your File and where you'd like to share it.

Creating Playlists and Listening to Music on iTunes

When you're ready to start playlist creation and music listening on iTunes, the first step is to launch the iTunes application on your MacBook Air or Pro. To do this, open Finder by clicking its icon in the dock at the bottom of your screen and then locate the iTunes app under Applications. Select it to open it.

Once iTunes is open, you will see a list of music featured on the iTunes Store. To find the songs in your iTunes library, click the Library tab at the top of the window. It will display all the media content you have purchased or imported to your computer.

Once you've found a song to add to a playlist, right-click on it to bring up the pop-up menu, select Add to Playlist from this menu and then select or create a new playlist.

To **create a new playlist**, click File on the menu bar at the top of the window and then choose New Playlist. Enter a name for your list and click the Create button.

To **add music to your playlist**, select the songs you want and drag them onto the playlist in the left menu. You can also click Edit then Add to Playlist on the pop-up menu when right-clicking on a song.

When your playlist is complete, double-click on it to listen, skip or go back to a song, and use the controls at the top of the window. You can create multiple playlists and then quickly switch between them by selecting them in the left menu.

Once you're done listening to your music, select File, then Quit iTunes in the menu bar to close the application. Now you know how to create playlists and listen to your music on iTunes using MacBook Air or Pro.

CHAPTER 13: ONLINE BANKING
AND SHOPPING

Security should always be a priority when it comes to online banking and shopping with your MacBook Air or Pro. That's why it's essential to take the proper steps to ensure that your information is safe when you use your laptop for these activities.

Before beginning online banking or shopping, ensure your wireless connection is secure. To do this, click on the Wi-Fi icon in the menu bar and select "Turn Wi-Fi On." You should also ensure your laptop is password protected, so no one else can access it without your permission.

When online banking or shopping, it's important to only use trusted websites verified by your bank or other financial institution. Always use HTTPS sites, as those are more secure than websites with just HTTP. When using a website for online banking or shopping, check that the web address starts with "https://" before entering any sensitive information into the form fields.

When making purchases online, be mindful of the potential risks of entering your payment information. If a website doesn't require you to enter personal information, it might not be secure. It's also essential to ensure that your credit card or bank account numbers are kept safe and never shared with anyone else.

When finished with online banking or shopping, always remember to log out of your accounts. It will help ensure that no one else can access your account from the same computer. Additionally, it's always a good idea to clear the browser history and delete any cookies on your MacBook Air or Pro after completing an online banking or shopping session.

By following these simple steps, you can ensure that your MacBook Air or Pro is secure when banking and shopping online. It will help to protect your personal information and keep your accounts safe.

Understanding Security for Online Transactions

The MacBook Air and Pro offer a safe and secure environment for online transactions. However, users must understand the steps involved in protecting their data when making purchases or other transactions through the internet. This guide will cover the essential security measures seniors should take to protect themselves while conducting online transactions with a MacBook Air or Pro.

Use Strong Passwords

Using strong and unique passwords when setting up an online account or making a purchase with your MacBook Air or Pro is essential. Avoid using common words, phrases, personal information (such as birthdays or addresses), and the same password across multiple accounts. Instead, opt for longer passwords that combine numbers, symbols, and both upper- and lower-case letters.

Use Two-Factor Authentication

Many online platforms offer two-factor authentication as an extra layer of security when making online transactions with your MacBook Air or Pro. It requires users to enter their username/password and provide additional information, such as a verification code sent to their phone.

Update Your Operating System

Regularly updating your MacBook Air or Pro's operating system is an important step in ensuring the security of your online transactions. It is especially true for seniors, who may need to become more familiar with the latest advancements in cybersecurity technology. Keeping up-to-date with the latest security patches and updates helps protect your data from hackers, viruses, and other malicious attacks.

Use a Virtual Private Network (VPN)

A VPN keeps your online activities secure when using your MacBook Air or Pro for online transactions. A VPN encrypts all the data that passes through it, making it virtually impossible for anyone to intercept your communication. It also protects your identity by masking your IP address and location.

Following these steps will help seniors remain safe and secure when conducting online transactions with their MacBook Air or Pro. By understanding the importance of strong passwords, two-factor authentication, regular system updates, and VPNs, seniors can have peace of mind when making purchases or other transactions online.

Making Purchases Easily & Securely

When it comes to shopping and banking online, seniors should be aware of the risks associated with these activities. Protecting yourself and your data is essential to keeping your financial information secure. This step-by-step guide will help you make safe and secure purchases on your MacBook Air or Pro.

First, you'll need to ensure your MacBook is updated with the latest security updates and anti-virus protection. The most recent versions of macOS have built-in protections to ward off malware and other malicious software. You'll want to be up-to-date before beginning online shopping or banking activities.

Once your MacBook is secure, it's time to start shopping. You'll first need to set up an online payment method, such as a PayPal account or credit card. Make sure you use a trusted and secure transaction method to protect your financial information.

Once you have your payment system set up, it's time to begin exploring the world of online shopping. You can start by visiting your favorite stores or searching the web for items you're interested in buying. When browsing, read any terms and conditions associated with the purchase before adding it to your cart.

When ready to checkout, look for a secure payment page with "https://" in the URL bar. It indicates that the store is using encryption to keep your information safe. Using only trusted payment methods, such as PayPal or a major credit card, is also important.

Finally, keep track of your online purchases and banking activities. Regularly check your account statements and credit reports for suspicious activity or unauthorized charges. This way, you can quickly identify and address any potential security issues.

Following these simple steps, you can confidently make secure purchases on your MacBook Air or Pro.

Managing Credit Card Information

Using a credit card is one of the easiest and most convenient purchases. However, it can also be dangerous if you don't manage your credit card information appropriately and securely. That's why it's important to know how to manage your credit card information effectively on your MacBook Air or Pro.

To start:

1. Open the "System Preference" application on your MacBook.
2. Select the "Security and Privacy" option from the System Preferences window.
3. Click the lock icon in the lower-left corner of the window to make changes.

Once you access the Security & Privacy settings, enable two-factor authentication for extra security. It will require an additional verification code whenever you make a purchase. You should also enable "Find My Mac" to locate your laptop if it is lost or stolen.

Next, open the "Keychain Access" application in System Preferences. It is where you will store all of your credit card information securely. Create a secure password for Keychain Access that only you know. Use a strong password with uppercase and lower-case letters, numbers, and symbols.

Now that Keychain Access is secure, add your credit card information: type in the cardholder's name, credit card number, expiration date, security code (CVV), and billing address. Be sure to double-check all the information before saving it.

Finally, you should use a password manager app like LastPass or 1Password to store your passwords and credit card credentials in one secure location. This way, you don't have to remember every single login and can access them easily with just one master password.

These simple steps allow you to quickly and securely manage your credit card information on your MacBook Air or Pro. It will help keep your credit safe and secure while allowing you to make purchases easily.

Be sure to review your security settings regularly to ensure that they are up-to-date. With the proper precautions, you can rest assured that your credit card information is safe and secure.

CHAPTER 14: THINGS TO KEEP IN MIND

When using a MacBook, it is crucial to be mindful of some safety practices:

1. Never leave your laptop unattended in public spaces; ensure that it is securely locked away when not used. It is also recommended to avoid using unsecured Wi-Fi networks or downloading untrusted software, as this could lead to malicious attacks on your computer.

2. Keeping the device clean and free of dust is vital by using canned air or a vacuum cleaner attachment to blow away any dirt or debris.

3. Back up all important data to an external hard drive or cloud storage regularly to protect it from potential loss due to hardware failure.

Moreover, keep the following points in mind.

Ergonomics & Accessibility

When using a MacBook Air or Pro, seniors need to pay special attention to ergonomics and accessibility. That's because as people age, their ability to use technology can become more challenging due to physical changes. Here are a few tips for ensuring you (or your loved one) get the most out of their laptop experience.

First, make sure to use an adjustable laptop stand and a separate keyboard and mouse since seniors have more difficulty with fine motor skills. It will help reduce strain on the hands, wrists, and shoulders while typing or navigating the features. If a separate keyboard isn't available, look for a laptop with a bigger keyboard, like the MacBook Air or Pro.

Second, adjust the laptop's display settings to make the text easier to read. Try increasing the font size or contrast, reducing brightness, and switching from a glossy screen to an anti-glare one (if available). Additionally, use software such as ZoomText or Magnifier to magnify the entire screen. Lastly, consider using voice-activated software such as Siri or Dragon NaturallySpeaking to help with tasks like sending emails and searching the web.

Finally, ensure that you (or your loved one) are comfortable using their laptop. That means setting up an ergonomic workspace and taking regular breaks. Consider using a laptop with adjustable angles to make viewing the screen at different levels easier. With these tips and tricks, seniors can enjoy their MacBook Air or Pro while minimizing potential physical discomfort.

Remember, when it comes to ergonomics and accessibility with a MacBook Air or Pro, it's essential to take the time to customize settings and check for physical comfort. With the right setup, seniors can enjoy a comfortable and productive experience with their laptops!

Choosing the Right Accessories

When selecting the right accessories for your MacBook Air or Pro, seniors should consider their computing needs and lifestyle. For example, if you are a senior who likes to travel frequently, invest in a lightweight laptop sleeve explicitly designed for carrying a laptop safely. If you want to work from home more often, purchase a wireless mouse and keyboard to work comfortably from anywhere.

Additionally, if your laptop battery is starting to show signs of weakening, consider purchasing an extended-life battery pack that will give your MacBook Air or Pro the extra boost it needs to keep up with your computing needs. Finally, if you are an avid music enthusiast or like to use your laptop for gaming, consider investing in a good pair of headphones or gaming headsets. It will allow you to enjoy hours of entertainment without disturbing those around you.

No matter what type of senior lifestyle you lead, there is sure to be the perfect set of accessories to help you make the most of your MacBook Air or Pro. Take the time to research and compare different options to ensure that you select the right accessories for your specific needs. This guide should provide a great starting point when deciding what laptop accessories will work best for your lifestyle.

Understanding iCloud Storage and Access

The iCloud drive is a cloud-based storage system offered by Apple that allows you to store and access your files, photos, videos, documents, music, and more on any Mac or iOS device. With iCloud Drive, you can easily share items with friends and family or collaborate on projects with colleagues. It's easy to keep your important files organized and accessible from anywhere.

With iCloud Drive, you can store up to 5 GB of data for free. If you need to store more than that, you can upgrade your storage plan to either 50 GB or 2 TB (the maximum). You can manage your storage in the Apple iCloud settings on your Mac or iOS device.

The iCloud drive also has an app for iOS and Mac to access your iCloud files. You can browse, search and view files in the iCloud Drive app and move them to other apps from within the iCloud Drive app.

If you're using a MacBook Air or Pro, you'll need to ensure your device is set up to use an iCloud drive. To do this, go to the System Preferences app on your Mac, and click on "iCloud." You can log in with your Apple ID and password and enable the iCloud drive. Once set up, any files you save in the iCloud Drive folder on your Mac will be automatically synced to your other devices.

The iCloud drive is a great way to keep your important documents, photos, and files organized and accessible from anywhere. Whether you're using a MacBook Air or Pro, it's easy to get an iCloud drive set up and start using it to store and share your files.

Setting Up External Hard Drives and Network Storage

Let's move on to setting up external hard drives and network storage in your MacBook Air or Pro. External hard drives are a great way to store large amounts of data without worrying about running out of space on your laptop. Additionally, if you have multiple computers, a network storage device can help keep them all safe and secure.

First, check to ensure that the hard drive you plan to use is compatible with your laptop. You will also want to ensure it has enough storage capacity for your data. Once you have chosen an external hard drive that meets these requirements, it's time to connect it to your MacBook Air or Pro.

For USB connections, plug the USB cable into the port on your laptop and then the other end into the drive. If you have a Thunderbolt connection, insert the appropriate adapter into your laptop's Thunderbolt port. Once connected, a prompt should appear asking if you want to use this device with Time Machine or as an external hard drive.

For network storage, you will need to connect your laptop to the same Wi-Fi or Ethernet connection as the device. If connecting via Wi-Fi, you must select the correct network and enter any required password information. Plug an Ethernet cable into your laptop and the device for Ethernet connections.

Once your external hard drive or network storage is connected, you can access and save files just as you would with any other folder. Enjoy the extra storage space!

With these steps, setting up an external hard drive or network storage for your MacBook Air or Pro should be a breeze. Now you can enjoy the convenience and security of extra storage space without taking up too much space on your laptop.

Sharing Files with Other Computers or Devices

Using your MacBook Air or Pro to share files with other computers and devices is a great way to keep all your information in one place. Here, I'll take you through the steps for setting up file sharing on your Mac with other Apple devices and accessing shared folders from Windows-based PCs.

For Mac-to-Mac sharing, you must connect your computer to the same network as the other Mac you wish to share with. To set up file sharing on your Mac:

1. Go to System Preferences > Sharing and select File Sharing in the list of services.
2. Check the box next to "File Sharing" if it isn't already checked.
3. Select the "Options..." button and choose who will access your shared folders.
4. Click on the "+" sign to add users, or remove them by selecting their name and clicking the "-" symbol.
5. Once you've set up users, click on the folder icon to choose which folders you want to share.
6. Select the individual folders and click "Add" next to them for them to appear under "Shared Folders."
7. Once you've selected your shared folders, make sure you have clicked "Done."

To access shared folders from a Windows-based PC:

1. On your Windows computer, open File Explorer and select Network on the left side of the window.
2. It will take time for your Mac to appear on the available computers or devices list.
3. Once your Mac appears, double-click on it to view the shared folders.
4. Select the folder you want to access and click "OK."

You will now be able to open and edit files in this folder as if they were stored on your computer's hard drive.

With these steps, you can easily access and share files with your Mac and other computers and devices. And remember to enable password protection for any shared folders that contain sensitive information!

The above steps provide a simple guide for setting up file sharing on your MacBook Air or Pro so you can share documents, photos, music, and more with other computers and devices. By following these steps, you can ensure that any sensitive data on your computer is kept secure while allowing easy access for people who need it. With file sharing enabled, you can easily keep up with friends, family, and colleagues no matter where they are.

CHAPTER 15: ACCESSORIZING
YOUR MACBOOK

When accessorizing your MacBook Air or Pro, there are plenty of options. Certain accessories may be more suitable than others depending on what you need and want from your MacBook. Here is a guide to help seniors make informed decisions when it comes to buying accessories for their MacBook Air or Pro:

Cases and Covers

Cases protect your MacBook from scratches and other damage. Choose a suit that fits the exact model of your MacBook to ensure proper protection.

Keyboard Protectors

If you use your laptop often, a keyboard protector is essential for keeping dirt, dust, and liquid away from the keys. Many keyboard protectors also feature backlighting or anti-glare properties.

Batteries and Chargers

Investing in a good-quality battery and charger is important. Look for ones specifically designed for your MacBook model, so you can be sure they will work perfectly.

Memory Cards and Storage

Many MacBook have limited storage space, so investing in external memory cards or storage devices may be necessary. Consider buying a card reader to help transfer files from your laptop to the storage device quickly and easily.

Docking Stations

Docking stations are great for connecting multiple devices to your laptop. It makes different managing devices and transferring data between them a breeze.

These tips help seniors make the most of their MacBook Air or Pro. With the right accessories, you can ensure your device is always working at its best!

Keeping Your MacBook Safe From Damage and Theft

When it comes to protecting your MacBook Air or Pro, there are a few items you can purchase to help keep it safe from damage and theft.

One of the most important accessories is a laptop bag or sleeve. It helps protect your computer from scratches and other forms of physical damage. It also offers an element of insulation to help keep your computer from overheating in extreme temperatures. Many laptop bags and sleeves come with additional pockets, which makes it easier to stay organized when traveling.

Anti-theft devices are also a great way to keep your MacBook safe from theft. These devices can be attached directly to the laptop or placed outside the bag or sleeve. Many of these devices make a loud noise when someone touches the laptop, which can deter thieves. Other anti-theft devices use GPS technology to track the location of your laptop if it is stolen.

If you take your MacBook with you, consider purchasing a surge protector or universal power adapter. These devices will help protect your computer from power surges, which can cause irreparable damage. Universal power adapters are handy if you travel abroad, as they allow you to plug in your laptop without worrying about compatibility issues.

Finally, screen protectors and keyboard covers are a great way to safeguard the display and keys from dirt and dust. They also help avoid permanent fingerprints from being left behind on your laptop, which can reduce its resale value.

Investing in the right accessories can keep your MacBook Air or Pro safe from damage and theft. Taking simple precautions will help ensure your laptop continues functioning for years.

CHAPTER 16: TROUBLESHOOTING YOUR MACBOOK AIR AND PRO

The MacBook Air and Pro are two of the most popular laptops on the market. They are sleek, powerful machines with many features and capabilities. However, they can be prone to common issues that require troubleshooting or repairs.

Identifying Common Problems

Troubleshooting common MacBook issues can be time-consuming, but ensuring that the laptop remains in top condition is necessary. With the right knowledge and attention to detail, you can solve even complex problems quickly and effectively. With the proper care, users can enjoy their MacBook for years.

The first step in troubleshooting common MacBook issues is to identify the problem. You can do it through a process of elimination involving inspecting the laptop's hardware and software components.

Hardware Issues

Hardware problems may include faulty or damaged parts such as fans, hard drives, keyboards, or other physical components. To address these issues, you should check all the cables and ports to ensure they are appropriately connected. If the case is still present, you may need to contact Apple Support for assistance or take your MacBook to an authorized repair shop for further inspection.

Software Problems

Software issues can range from corrupted system files to incompatible software or drivers. To identify software issues, users should check for updates in their MacBook's operating system and any additional programs they may have installed. If no updates are available, users should check if any settings have been changed or changed back to the default configuration.

A thorough examination of the laptop's internal components will be necessary in some cases. It may include taking apart the casing and inspecting all internal parts for signs of damage or corrosion. If any potential issues are identified, you should address these as soon as possible.

Determining the Source

After the hardware and software components have been thoroughly inspected and identified, the next step is to determine the source of the problem. Depending on the issue's complexity, it may require additional research or consultation with a technician. Once the source has been determined, users can begin to take steps to correct it.

Check for Updates

System updates are an important part of maintaining your MacBook Air or Pro. They help keep your system running while providing the latest security patches and bug fixes. You should regularly check for available updates every week.

To do this, open the App Store from the dock at the bottom of your screen. Then click the Updates icon at the top-left of the window. It will show you all available software updates for your MacBook Air or Pro and any third-party apps you may install.

If there are any updates available, click Update All to install them. It is important to keep up to date with the latest operating system version, as this will help protect you against security threats.

You should also check for firmware updates in System Preferences. These updates may be necessary depending on your MacBook Air or Pro age. Firmware updates can improve performance and battery life and provide enhanced security features.

It is essential to regularly check for updates to ensure that your MacBook Air or Pro is functioning optimally and that you are protected against security threats. Keep in mind that it can take some time for the updates to install, so it is best to do this when you are not in a rush.

If you have questions or concerns about system updates, contact Apple Support for more information. They will be able to help you find the best update solutions for your MacBook Air or Pro.

Additional Note: Remember to restart your MacBook Air or Pro after installing updates. It will help ensure that the updates take effect and all changes have been properly applied.

Restarting your MacBook Air or Pro

It often helps clear up any software glitches preventing the device from working properly. It's also important to check for any available system updates after restarting, as they may address any issues you're experiencing.

If you still have problems with your MacBook, try running an antivirus scan to check for any potential viruses or malware that may be affecting it. Many free and paid options are available to help keep your computer safe from malicious software.

Fan Running Constantly

Several things, such as a blocked air vent or an overheating processor, can cause it. To resolve this, check your air vents for blockages and make sure your laptop is properly ventilated. If the fan is still running at high speeds, you may need to clean out any dust and debris clogging up the fan blades.

Corrupted Operating System.

It can occur when a virus or malware has infected your laptop, causing it to run slower than usual. To address this issue, you should run a virus scan and make sure your security software is up-to-date. You may need to reinstall the operating system or contact Apple Support for assistance if the issue persists.

Display Issues

It is common to experience display problems with MacBook Air or Pro. The most frequent symptom is that the screen appears dimmer than usual. However, other symptoms may include lines across the screen, flickering, distorted colors and images, and a black or blank screen. Fortunately, there are multiple solutions for trying to fix these issues.

Restarting the computer may help to fix the problem, or you can try adjusting the brightness settings and calibrating the display. For more serious issues, resetting

NVRAM (Non-Volatile Random-Access Memory) and PRAM (Parameter RAM) may be necessary. If all else fails, you should consult a technician for further assistance.

System Overheating

MacBook Air and Pro can sometimes experience overheating due to faulty or outdated hardware, dust accumulation on cooling fans, or running too many applications simultaneously. To fix this problem, the user should check for software updates, clean out dust from the fans, close unused programs and disable unnecessary browser add-ons. For more extreme cases, the user may need to take the laptop to a technician for further diagnosis.

Moreover, it can be due to heavy software usage or an old battery that needs replacing. To prevent overheating, check for unused apps running in the background and disable them.

You should also check for dust build-up on the vents of your laptop and clean them if needed. Additionally, you should ensure that it is running the latest version of macOS and all its updates. You might also need to reset the System Management Controller (SMC) on your MacBook. To do this, turn off your computer and then press and hold the left Shift + Control + Option keys and the power button for 10-15 seconds. After releasing these buttons, restart your laptop to check if the overheating problem has been resolved.

Battery Issues

Over time, MacBook Air or Pro batteries can start to drain quickly or not charge at all. To try and fix this problem, the user should calibrate their battery by running it down completely and then setting it back up again. If this does not work, the user should try resetting the SMC (System Management Controller) and PRAM (Parameter RAM). If the issue persists, then replacing the battery may be necessary.

If your MacBook Air or Pro has poor battery life, go to the Apple menu and select System Preferences > Energy Saver. Make sure that "Processor Performance" is set to "Better performance" instead of "Higher Efficiency." You should also check for unused apps running in the background and disable them. Additionally, you may need to reset the System Management Controller to restore optimal battery performance. To do this, turn off your computer and then press and hold the left Shift + Control + Option keys and the power button for 10-15 seconds. After releasing these buttons, restart your laptop to check if the battery life has improved.

Keyboard Issues

Malfunctioning keyboards are another common problem for MacBook Air and Pro users. Before trying more drastic measures, the user should check if their keyboard is damaged or dirty and clean it as necessary. If this does not work, resetting the SMC (System Management Controller) may help fix the issue. For more extreme cases, replacing the entire keyboard may be necessary.

Unresponsive Touchpad

MacBook Air and Pro computers are built with a highly sensitive touchpad. Suppose the cursor needs to respond more quickly to your fingers. In that case, you can try disabling "Force Click" from the System Preferences menu. You should also ensure that your laptop is running the latest macOS version and all its updates.

You must reset the System Management Controller (SMC) on your MacBook. To do this, turn off your computer and then press and hold the left Shift + Control + Option keys and the power button for 10-15 seconds. After releasing these buttons, restart your laptop to check if the touchpad is responding correctly.

Slow Performance

If your MacBook Air or Pro is running slow, you should check for any unused apps running in the background and disable them. Additionally, you should ensure that your laptop is running the latest version of macOS and all its updates. You might also need to reset the System Management Controller (SMC) on your MacBook.

To do this, turn off your computer and then press and hold the left Shift + Control + Option keys and the power button for 10-15 seconds. After releasing these buttons, restart your laptop to check if the performance has improved.

Low Storage Space

Suppose you frequently receive notifications that your MacBook Air or Pro is running out of storage. In that case, it's time to delete unused apps and files on your laptop. You can also purchase a larger external hard drive to store your data and free up some space on your computer.

You should also check for any software updates available and download them if needed, as this may help to improve storage capacity.

Finally, you can try resetting the System Management Controller (SMC) on your MacBook. To do this, turn off your computer and then press and hold the left Shift + Control + Option keys and the power button for 10-15 seconds. After releasing these buttons, restart your laptop to check if it has more storage space.

These are some of the most common problems that can occur on a MacBook Air or Pro and how you can fix them. By following these steps, you can resolve any issues you might be having with your laptop. If you're still having trouble, it's best to consult an expert or contact Apple support for help.

Troubleshooting Internet Connection Problems

First, check to make sure that the Wi-Fi is turned on. Open up System Preferences and click on network. Check the box next to "Enable Wi-Fi" if it isn't already checked. Try rebooting the system if the Wi-Fi is enabled and still not connecting.

If a reboot doesn't solve the problem, open up System Preferences again and ensure you are connected to the correct network. If you are trying to connect to a password-protected network, ensure you enter the right credentials.

If you still have trouble connecting, try resetting your Network Settings by going to the Apple menu and clicking 'Restart.' Once restarted, go to System Preferences again and click on network. Select "Reset Network Settings" at the bottom of the window. It will reset your Network Settings and may solve the issue.

Moreover, try contacting your internet service provider or Apple Support for further assistance. They will be able to help you troubleshoot any issues you're having and get your connection up and running again.

Understanding Error Messages

Understanding Error Messages in MacBook Air or Pro can be daunting, especially if you are unfamiliar with the functions of your laptop. To help guide you through this process, we've created a step-by-step guide that will walk you through what to look for and how to interpret the messages provided.

First, we'll look at the error messages you can encounter on your Mac. These are usually displayed in an alert box, along with a brief explanation of the issue. Examples include:

- *"An unexpected error occurred"*
- *"This application quit unexpectedly."*
- *"The application cannot be opened due to a problem."*

Once you've identified the type of error message, it's time to troubleshoot! A good starting point is to open System Information and check for any reported hardware or software issues. It can give helpful insight into what may have caused the problem. You can also check the Console app for potential errors.

After you've identified the error's source, it's time to take action! One of the best ways to do this is to reinstall any software or hardware you used when the error occurred. It will help reset any settings that may have been causing a conflict or malfunction. Try a Safe Boot to check for any potential software issues.

Finally, contact Apple Support for assistance if you still can't resolve the issue. They will be able to provide you with personalized help and advice on how to troubleshoot your MacBook Air or Pro.

Following these steps should ensure you have the best experience with your MacBook Air or Pro. With patience and troubleshooting, you can learn to understand error messages with names on Mac laptops and find solutions quickly!

Testing and Restoring Your System Settings

Once you have successfully tested and restored your system settings, there are additional steps to ensure that all processes run smoothly.

First, make sure to check for any updates that may be available for your MacBook Air or Pro. It is crucial because it will help keep your computer running optimally and avoid any potential problems in the future. To do this, open the App Store and select "Updates" from the menu. From here, you can see if there are any updates available for your system.

Second, clean up any unnecessary files that may take up space on your device. It includes redundant copies of documents or files that you no longer need. You can also uninstall any applications that you no longer use. To do this, select the app and click "Uninstall."

Finally, back up your data regularly. It includes documents, photos, music, and other files that are important to you. Having a backup of your data will help ensure that it is safe and secure in the case of a system failure.

These simple steps will help keep your MacBook Air or Pro running smoothly and optimally. By regularly testing and restoring your system settings, keeping it up to date, and cleaning out any unnecessary files, you can ensure that you get the best performance from your device.

Understanding the Recovery Process For More Serious Issues

The first step in recovery from more severe issues with MacBook Air or Pro is to back up your data. You can do it through Apple's Time Machine feature, which allows you to easily make copies of your important files and folders to retrieve them if anything goes wrong with your device. If you have never used Time Machine before, you can follow the instructions on Apple's support page to set it up and get started.

Once your data is backed up, you should attempt to restart your computer. Hold the power button on the top right side of your MacBook for a few seconds until it turns off. If this does not work, you may need to press and hold the power button for ten seconds or more. After your computer is turned off, turn it on and see if the issue is resolved.

If restarting your MacBook doesn't fix the issue, try using Apple's Disk Utility tool to diagnose and repair any potential problems. To do this, open the Disk Utility app from your applications folder and select the MacBook drive you want to check for errors. Click the "Verify" button to scan your hard drive for any issues, and click "Repair Disk Permissions" if any errors are found.

If the issue remains unresolved, you may need to reset your MacBook's system management controller (SMC). To do this, shut down your computer and unplug all external devices and power cables. Next, press and hold the left Shift + Control + Option keys on the keyboard and the power button simultaneously for about 10 seconds. After that, release all keys and the power button and plug in the power cable again. Finally, press the power button to turn on your MacBook and see if the issue is resolved.

Suppose you encounter any difficulties during the recovery process. In that case, you should contact Apple Support or a certified repair specialist to help you out. With their assistance, you should be able to get your MacBook Air or Pro back up and running in no time.

CHAPTER 17: KEEPING THE
MACBOOK SECURE

For seniors, having a secure MacBook Air or Pro is essential. With the advent of technology and its rapid evolution, it can take time to keep up with the latest security measures needed to protect your device. This guide aims to educate seniors on protecting their MacBook from potential threats and keeping them secure.

MacBook Air and Pro are the most popular laptops on the market. As technology evolves, it becomes increasingly important to ensure that our computers stay secure. It is especially true for seniors who may be more vulnerable to online threats. Fortunately, various security options are available for MacBook Air and Pro users that can help keep their data and personal information safe.

Built-in Security Features

MacBook Air and Pro have several built-in security features that make them ideal for seniors. The macOS operating system is designed to protect users' data and privacy while allowing them to explore their digital world safely.

Password Protection

A strong password is the most basic form of security available for MacBook Air and Pro users. Choosing a complex, unique password that cannot be easily guessed by hackers or malicious software will go a long way toward protecting your device. It's also important to never share your passwords with anyone else and to frequently change them.

FileVault

FileVault is a great tool for seniors who want to keep their data secure on their MacBook Air or Pro. It encrypts the entire contents of a hard disk, including all documents, photos, and videos, providing enhanced security.

Not only does it protect against physical theft and tampering, but it also safeguards all data in case of hardware failure or accidental deletion. Since passwords are difficult for seniors to remember and type, FileVault offers multi-factor authentication options like Touch ID for added security. FileVault is easy to set up and use on a Mac, making it an ideal solution for older users who want to keep their data secure. With this reliable and intuitive tool, seniors can rest assured that their data is protected and private.

And when they need help understanding how to use FileVault, they can easily find many online resources with step-by-step guides and tutorials. With a few clicks and some simple instructions, seniors can be sure that their data is secure. If you or an elderly family member wants to protect their data, FileVault is the perfect solution. It offers strong encryption that can help keep your data secure and private.

Secure Erase

Secure Erase for MacBook Air and Pro is essential for seniors who want to keep their data safe. With Secure Erase, all the sensitive information on your MacBook will be permanently erased in a matter of minutes, ensuring that no one can access it without your permission.

Secure Erase for MacBook Air and Pro also helps protect against viruses, malware, and other malicious software by wiping out any files or programs installed on your system. It is a must-have feature for seniors concerned about their data security.

It is user-friendly, making it easy for seniors to take advantage of its security benefits. The program is designed to be intuitive and simple to use, allowing even the most computer-shy seniors to understand how it works quickly. It also has various helpful tutorials that can help guide users through the setup process.

Overall, Secure Erase is a must-have feature for seniors who want the highest level of data security possible. With it, they can rest assured that their sensitive information is safe from hackers and viruses.

Third-Party Security Software

Third-Party Security Software in MacBook Air and Pro is designed to protect seniors from the ever-changing landscape of online threats. It provides comprehensive protection against viruses, malware, phishing attacks, identity theft, and other malicious activities threatening a senior's online security. With third-party security software installed and regularly updated, seniors can be sure that their data and financial information are safe from cybercriminals. Seniors can also be assured that their online activity is being monitored so that you can detect any suspicious or malicious activity immediately.

Antivirus and Anti-malware Solutions

MacBook Air and Pro are great options for seniors, especially when protecting their devices from malicious software. It is important to set up antivirus and anti-malware solutions on these machines to ensure maximum protection.

Antivirus software scans the entire system for potential virus threats. It will detect any existing infections and, if necessary, delete the malicious programs. You can also use antivirus software to block malicious websites and emails from entering your system.

Anti-malware solutions use various techniques, including signature matching, heuristics, and behavior monitoring, to identify and block malicious programs before they can do any damage.

It is vital to ensure you have the latest, up-to-date antivirus and anti-malware software installed on your MacBook Air or Pro. It will ensure that your device is protected from any new threats that may arise. Additionally, you should regularly scan your system with these programs to make sure all threats have been eliminated.

Multi-factor Authentication Solutions

Using multi-factor authentication solutions in MacBook Air and Pro is essential for seniors who want to secure their data, accounts, and personal information. It adds an extra layer of security by requiring the user to provide more than one form of authentication to access their device or account. It helps protect against hackers, phishing attempts, and other malicious activities.

There are a few options available regarding multi-factor authentication solutions for seniors using MacBook Air and Pro. Using biometrics such as fingerprint or facial recognition offers an easy and secure way to log in without remembering complex passwords or passphrases. Some multi-factor authentication options also allow users to set up a trusted device, such as their Apple Watch or iPhone, as an additional form of authentication.

Another option is two-factor authentication (2FA). It is typically used when logging into websites and accounts requiring two identification forms. It often involves something the user knows (such as a password) and something the user has (such as a phone or token). It adds an extra security layer to ensure that only authorized users can access the account.

Finally, seniors using MacBook Air and Pro can also utilize device management software such as Find My Mac, which allows them to track their device if it ever gets lost or stolen. It can be a great way to protect their data and personal information if their laptop is no longer in their possession.

Overall, using multi-factor authentication solutions for seniors on MacBook Air and Pro is essential for protecting their data and accounts from malicious activities. By taking advantage of biometric authentication, 2FA, and device management software, seniors can enjoy the benefits of a secure online environment while using their devices.

Encryption Software

For seniors using a MacBook Air or Pro, encryption software is crucial for keeping their data secure. There are several types of encryption software available for Macs. Each type offers different levels of security and features depending on the user's needs.

The most common type of encryption software for Macs is FileVault, which is part of macOS and works with the latest operating system versions. FileVault encrypts an individual's files and folders, making them inaccessible to anyone else without a password or encryption key. It provides strong security against potential attackers and a convenient way to secure data locally.

Another type of encryption software for Macs is disk encryption software, which encrypts the entire hard drive of a Mac. This type of encryption is more comprehensive than FileVault. It can provide enhanced security against attacks that target the startup process or other areas where data is not encrypted.

Finally, there are third-party encryption programs that you can use to provide additional levels of security. These programs can encrypt files and folders with various algorithms, making them even more difficult for attackers to access or decode. They also often have other valuable features, such as automatic backups and strong password protection.

No matter which type of encryption software you choose, it's important to back up any encrypted data regularly. It will help ensure that the user still has access to their files and information if a device is lost or stolen. It is also important to remember that no matter how secure your data may be, it can still be vulnerable if someone gains physical access to your Mac. Taking extra steps to protect the device, such as using a secure password, is important for overall safety and security.

With the right encryption software, seniors can enjoy added protection while using their MacBook Air or Pro. Whether they choose FileVault, disk encryption software, or third-party programs, having the right encryption software in place can help keep their data secure and provide peace of mind.

CHAPTER 18: BEST PRACTICES FOR KEEPING YOUR MACBOOK SECURE

Keeping your MacBook secure is essential if you're using it to store sensitive information or handle financial transactions. With the right security measures, you can prevent hackers from accessing your data and protect yourself from online threats. In the following paragraphs, we'll explore some best practices for securing your MacBook.

Enable Automatic Updates

Enabling automatic updates for your MacBook is a great way to ensure that the software on your device is always up-to-date. It will help protect your system against vulnerabilities, as Apple regularly releases new patches and fixes. By enabling automatic updates, you won't have to remember to download and install them manually — they will be done for you automatically.

Here's how to get started:

1. Click the Apple icon in the top left of your screen and select System Preferences
2. Select Software Update from the list on the left side of the window
3. Check "Automatically keep my Mac up to date."
4. Set the frequency you would like updates to be installed (daily, weekly or monthly)
5. Click "Install system data files and security updates."
6. Your MacBook will automatically install software updates when they become available, keeping your device secure.
7. When an update is at hand, you will see a notification, and you can choose to install it now or later.

By enabling automatic updates for your MacBook, you'll ensure that your device is always running the latest software with the latest security patches installed, keeping it secure from potential vulnerabilities. So, make sure to keep this setting enabled and stay up to date!

Use Strong and Unique Passwords

It is important to create passwords for your MacBook that are strong and unique. Strong passwords include a combination of uppercase and lowercase letters, numbers, and symbols. The longer the password, the stronger it will be.

Avoiding common words or phrases is important, as hackers can easily guess these. It is also essential to avoid using the same password for multiple accounts, as this significantly increases your risk of being hacked.

Consider creating a passkey or code system if you have to use the same password for multiple online accounts. Finally, make sure to update your passwords regularly and keep them confidential.

Store them in a secure location such as an encrypted file or password manager. Following these best practices ensures that your MacBook remains secured and protected against malicious attacks.

Set Up Login Notifications

Login notifications are an essential security measure for anyone using a MacBook. They alert you when someone has logged into your account, allowing you to take any necessary action if the login is unauthorized. To set up login notifications on your MacBook, follow these steps:

1. Click the Apple menu in the upper-left corner of the screen and select "System Preferences."
2. Select "Users & Groups" in the System Preferences window, then click the padlock icon in the lower-left corner of the window to unlock it. You will be prompted to enter your MacBook password at this point.
3. Click on your username in the users' list, then click the "Change Password..." button.
4. Choose a secure password for your account, then check the box next to "Show a message when the screen is locked or when logging in," and enter a custom message of your choice.
5. Click "OK" to save your changes and close the window.

That's it! You have successfully set up login notifications on your MacBook. Now, you'll be alerted whenever someone logs into your account and can take immediate action if the login is unauthorized.

Back-Up Data Regularly

It's essential to back up your data regularly, especially using a MacBook. A secure backup plan can help protect your files in case of hardware failure, malicious software attacks, or other unexpected events.

You can use Apple's Time Machine tool to create backups of your computer or save individual files and folders. Consider using an external hard drive or cloud storage service if you have large data.

You can also use disk cloning software to create an exact copy of your MacBook's hard drive, including all its settings and applications. Additionally, ensure you encrypt any backups you store offsite for added security. Doing this will help ensure that your data remains safe and secure.

Use Care When Surfing the Web

When using the internet on your MacBook, it is vital to take extra steps to keep yourself secure. Here are some simple tips and best practices for safe online browsing:

Avoid Clicking On Links From Unknown Sources.

If you receive an email or message from someone you don't know, be wary of clicking on any links they provide. Remember that you can easily disguise malicious websites to look like legitimate ones. If you need to figure out the source, it's best to err on caution.

Don't Enter Sensitive or Personal Information.

Be careful about entering sensitive pieces of data, such as passwords or credit card numbers, on websites you don't trust. If the site doesn't use a secure connection, it may be best to avoid entering personal data altogether.

Be Aware of Phishing Scams.

Phishing scams are attempts by malicious actors to trick people into entering their personal information in exchange for something they don't get. Be aware of emails and messages that may look legitimate but ask for your personal information – this is often a sign of a phishing scam.

Install Antivirus Software

It's crucial to have reliable antivirus software installed on your MacBook to protect you from viruses, malware, and other malicious code. Make sure to keep it up-to-date, as new threats are constantly emerging.

Following these simple tips can go a long way in keeping your device and data secure while you surf the web. If you're unsure of a website or link, remember that it's better to be safe than sorry.

Use a VPN When Connecting to Public Wi-Fi Networks

Connecting to public Wi-Fi networks without a virtual private network (VPN) can be risky. Unsecured public Wi-Fi networks make it easy for hackers to access your device's data and personal information and intercept communications.

A VPN creates an encrypted connection between your device and the internet, creating a secure tunnel for your data to travel through. It helps protect against potential bad actors from gaining access to your information or spying on unencrypted communications. Other benefits of VPN use include improved privacy, better access to blocked content, and faster streaming speeds.

When shopping for a VPN, look for one that is reliable and compatible with your MacBook. Look for a provider with strong encryption protocols, unlimited bandwidth, plenty of server locations, and a good customer support system. A good VPN should provide you with the highest level of security without sacrificing performance or speed.

VPN is the best way to protect yourself when connecting to public Wi-Fi networks. It will help keep your data secure, reduce the risk of cyber-attacks, and give you access to content you may block in specific countries or regions. Using a reliable VPN service, you can feel safe and secure using any public Wi-Fi network.

Don't Click On Suspicious Links or Attachments

It is important to be aware of unsolicited emails, messages, or links from unknown sources. Even if a link looks legitimate or seems harmless, it could potentially contain malicious software that can compromise the security of your MacBook. As such, it is best practice not to click on any suspicious links or attachments you receive via email or any other form of communication.

If you receive a link or attachment that prompts you to enter personal information, such as bank account numbers or passwords, be extra cautious and avoid clicking or downloading the attachment at all costs. It is likely an attempt to steal your information and should be reported immediately.

It is also important to be aware of phishing emails, deceitful messages that often appear to come from a legitimate source and contain malicious links or attachments. If you receive an email asking you to confirm your username and password, check the sender's address before responding. If the email does not seem authentic, report it as spam or delete it immediately.

Data Backup & Recovery Options

Data backup is essential to help protect your MacBook Air or Pro from data loss. It ensures that all your most important files will be safe and easily retrievable if anything happens to your computer. Many options exist for seniors looking for a reliable way to keep their data secure, such as using external hard drives, cloud storage services, and more.

External Hard Drives

External hard drives are an excellent option for backing up data. They can be plugged into any computer with USB ports and provide large storage space. They also come in different sizes and prices to suit your needs. The advantage is that you own the hardware and can access the data without an internet connection. However, it is important to ensure that you keep your external hard drive safe and away from water or heat sources, as these can damage the device.

Cloud Storage Services

Cloud storage services are becoming increasingly popular and are often provided by companies such as Google Drive, Microsoft One Drive, and Dropbox. These services store data on remote servers, meaning you can access them wherever you have an internet connection. They also provide increased security with encryption technology to protect your data from unauthorized access. However, they cost more than external hard drives and usually have limited storage space.

Time Machine

MacOS Time Machine is the built-in backup feature for a MacBook. It can back up your entire system, including all the files and applications installed on your computer. Time Machine is easy to use and automatically saves multiple copies of your data at regular intervals. Additionally, it is free to use as long as you have an external hard drive or other storage device connected.

By taking the time to back up your MacBook Air or Pro, you can ensure that all of your necessary data is secure and easily retrievable. With various options available, seniors should be able to find the best solution for their needs.

The bottom line is that data backup in MacBook Air and Pro is essential for seniors to protect their data and devices. With the right tools, such as external hard drives, cloud storage services, and Time Machine, they can be confident that their most important files will remain secure.

So, if you're a senior looking to back up your MacBook Air or Pro, consider these options and make sure you have a reliable way to protect your data.

By taking the time and effort to back up your data, you can be sure that all your important information will remain safe and secure!

Recovery Options

MacBook Air and Pro offer seniors a variety of recovery options. In both models, Apple provides an inbuilt Recovery Mode that you can access by restarting the computer and holding down Command-R until the Apple logo appears on the screen. This mode allows users to reinstall macOS or restore from a Time Machine backup, which can help seniors easily recover their lost data. MacBook Air and Pro models come preloaded with a built-in Internet Recovery Mode that you can access by restarting the computer and holding down the Option-Command-R keys until the Apple logo appears on the screen. This mode allows users to reinstall macOS without physical media and access Apple-provided software or firmware updates. Finally, both models have a Recovery Partition that you can access by restarting the computer and holding down the Option until the Recovery Partition menu appears on the screen.

This mode gives seniors access to various utilities such as Disk Utility, Terminal, and Firmware Password Utility, which can help them troubleshoot and fix common problems with their Mac. With these recovery options, seniors can rest assured that their MacBook Air or Pro will function if anything goes wrong.

CHAPTER 19: FREQUENTLY ASKED QUESTIONS

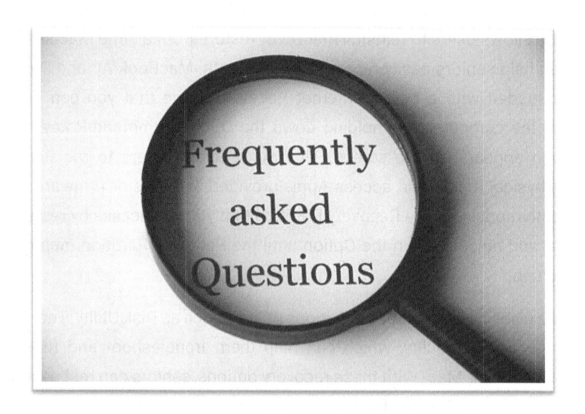

What is the best way to keep MacBook Air or Pro secure?

Keeping your MacBook Air or Pro secure is essential to protect your data and personal information. It would help if you used a strong password and two-factor authentication whenever possible. Additionally, installing anti-malware programs on your device and ensuring your operating system and apps are up-to-date with the latest security patches is essential. Finally, it's important to back up the data on your computer regularly. It ensures that you have stored a copy of your valuable files if anything happens to your MacBook Air or Pro.

How can I extend the battery life of my MacBook Air or Pro?

One of the best ways to extend your battery life is to reduce the brightness of your display when possible and avoid running power-intensive applications for long periods. Additionally, ensure that you keep your operating system and apps up-to-date with the latest security patches, as this can help reduce battery drain. Finally, consider using your device in power-saving mode whenever possible. It will limit some features and apps to conserve battery life.

What is the best way to clean my MacBook Air or Pro?

Keeping your MacBook Air or Pro clean is essential to prevent dust, dirt, and debris from damaging the internal components. The best way to clean the outside of your device is to lightly dampen a lint-free cloth with water, then gently wipe away any dirt or grime that has accumulated on the surface of your device. You should never use cleaning products or solvents on your device, as these could damage the finish. Additionally, clean out your device's ports and vents regularly with a can of compressed air. It will help keep dust and debris from clogging up the internal components.

What software is available for my MacBook Air or Pro?

Your MacBook Air or Pro comes pre-loaded with various software, including the popular macOS operating system. Additionally, many applications are available from the App Store and other online sources. Popular Apple-made apps include Pages, Numbers, and Keynote, while third-party apps can vary in purpose and price. No matter what software you need, something will likely be available for your device.

What accessories do I need for my MacBook Air or Pro?

Depending on how you plan to use your MacBook Air or Pro, there are a variety of accessories that could be beneficial. For example, an external mouse or keyboard can be helpful if you use your device for gaming. Additionally, you'll need the appropriate cables or adapters to connect other devices, such as a printer or scanner. Finally, if portability is essential to you, consider investing in a protective carrying case or backpack. It will keep your device safe from drops and bumps while you're on the go.

Can I upgrade my MacBook Air or Pro?

In some cases, upgrading specific components of your MacBook Air or Pro may be possible. For example, depending on your exact model, you can upgrade the RAM or storage capacity. However, it's important to keep in mind that opening up your device can void the warranty, so it's recommended that you only attempt upgrades if you are comfortable doing so. Additionally, it's important to ensure that any components you purchase are compatible with your exact model.

What should I do if my MacBook Air or Pro stops working?

If your device suddenly stops working, the first step is to power it off and then back on again. If this doesn't resolve the issue, take your device to an Apple store or authorized service center for diagnosis and repair. Additionally, if you're still under warranty, take advantage of that coverage to receive free repairs or replacements for any issues with your device.

What other tips should I remember while using my MacBook Air or Pro?

It's always a good idea to back up your data if something goes wrong. Please keep all your software updated to ensure your device runs correctly. Finally, if you're unsure about how a program or feature works, take some time to explore the help files or search for tutorials online—plenty of resources are available to help you get the most out of your MacBook Air or Pro.

Are there any special features tailored to seniors?

Yes! Several features are designed specifically with seniors in mind. For example, the larger text makes it easier to read on the screen, and Voice Over allows you to use voice commands to navigate your Mac. There is also a built-in magnifying glass tool to make the reading smaller text easier. You can customize all of these features in the System Preferences.

Additionally, Siri allows you to ask questions and get help hands-free. You can also use the "Do Not Disturb" mode when you don't want to be bothered by notifications. Finally, AppleCare has a special team dedicated to providing technical support for seniors. You can contact them at any time for assistance with your MacBook.

Is there a way to make the trackpad easier to use?

Yes! You can adjust the tracking speed, acceleration, and scrolling settings in System Preferences. You can also enable Tap to Click, which allows you to click by simply pressing down lightly on the trackpad. Finally, AppleCare has a special team dedicated to providing technical support for seniors that can help you adjust settings or troubleshoot any issues. You can contact them at any time for assistance with your MacBook.

Is there an easy way to safeguard my files?

Yes! iCloud automatically stores all your files, documents, photos, and more, making them easy to access from any Apple device. Additionally, you can enable FileVault encryption in System Preferences to protect sensitive information. It ensures your files are safe if you ever lose your Mac or share it with someone else. Finally, you can back up your files to an external hard drive or cloud storage for extra protection. You can also use the Time Machine feature to create backups of your Mac at regular intervals automatically.

CONCLUSION

The MacBook is an excellent choice for providing seniors with a dependable and user-friendly computer. It offers a robust operating system, intuitive design, and an array of helpful features that make it perfect for seniors new to using computers or those looking to upgrade their equipment. Its affordability makes it even more attractive, making it a great choice for those on a budget. The MacBook's wide range of applications makes it even more suitable. It gives seniors the tools to remain connected to family and friends, stay up-to-date on news and events, enjoy entertainment, and pursue hobbies or interests. In conclusion, the MacBook is an ideal choice for seniors who need a reliable, user-friendly, and affordable computer. With its robust operating system, helpful features, wide range of applications, and low cost, the MacBook is an excellent choice for seniors looking to stay connected in the digital age.

The MacBook has been designed with seniors in mind. It provides users with everything they need for effective and efficient computing. It is highly recommended for seniors, as it offers a great balance between value and usability. The MacBook provides seniors with an easy-to-use platform that is powerful and intuitive, allowing them to stay connected with their families, participate in activities, pursue new interests, and more. With its affordable price tag and wide array of features, the MacBook is an excellent choice for seniors who need a dependable computer.

In conclusion, Apple's MacBook Air and Pro are great options for seniors who want reliable performance from their computers. The Air is perfect for those who don't need a lot of power and are looking for something lightweight that won't weigh them down on the go. The Pro offers more performance, storage, and portability for those needing extra power and flexibility. Ultimately, both models are great options with plenty of features to choose from, so seniors should consider their needs before making a purchase decision.

So, if you're looking for a reliable and user-friendly laptop for yourself or someone else, the MacBook is worth considering. Its wide range of features makes it perfect for seniors new to computing or those looking to upgrade their equipment. The MacBook will provide many years of enjoyment and productivity with its robust operating system and intuitive design. The MacBook is worth considering if you're looking for a dependable laptop that will give you years of reliable performance.

Made in the USA
Las Vegas, NV
11 October 2023

78937697R00070